NO LONGER PROPERTY OF
SEATTLE PUBLIC LIBRARY

WHO'S QUALIFIED?

"New Democracy Forum operates at a level of literacy and responsibility which is all too rare in our time." —John Kenneth Galbraith

Other books in the NEW DEMOCRACY FORUM series:

WHO'S QUALIFIED?

LANI GUINIER AND SUSAN STURM

BEACON PRESS
BOSTON

BEACON PRESS
25 Beacon Street
Boston, Massachusetts 02108-2892
www.beacon.org

Beacon Press books
are published under the auspices of
the Unitarian Universalist Association of Congregations.

© 2001 by Beacon Press

ALL RIGHTS RESERVED
Printed in the United States of America

05 04 03 02 01   8 7 6 5 4 3 2 1

This book is printed on acid-free paper that meets the uncoated paper
ANSI/NISO specifications for permanence as revised in 1992.

Composition by Wilsted & Taylor Publishing Services

Library of Congress Cataloging-in-Publication Data

Guinier, Lani.
  Who's qualified? / Lani Guinier and Susan Sturm.
      p. cm—(New democracy forum)
  ISBN 0-8070-4335-4 (pbk. : alk. paper)
  1. Affirmative action programs—United States. 2. Employee
selection—United States. 3. Universities and colleges—United
States—Admission. I. Sturm, Susan. II. Title. III. Series.
  HF5549.5.A34 G85 2001
  331.13'3'0973—dc21

CONTENTS

3

1

THE FUTURE OF AFFIRMATIVE ACTION

SUSAN STURM AND LANI GUINIER

For more than two decades, affirmative action has been under sustained assault. In courts, legislatures, and the media, opponents have condemned it as an unprincipled program of racial and gender preferences that threatens fundamental American values of fairness, equality, and democratic opportunity. Such preferences, they say, are extraordinary departures from prevailing "meritocratic" modes of selection, which they present as both fair and functional: fair, because they treat all candidates as equals; functional, because they are well suited to picking the best candidates.

This challenge to affirmative action has met with concerted response. Defenders argue that affirmative action is still needed to rectify continued exclusion and marginalization. And they marshal considerable evidence showing that conventional standards of selection exclude women and people of color, and that people who were excluded in the past do not yet operate on a level playing field. But this response has largely been reactive. Proponents typically treat affirmative action as a crucial but peripheral supplement to

{ 3 }

an essentially sound framework of selection for jobs and schools.

We think it is time to shift the terrain of debate. We need to situate the conversation about race, gender, and affirmative action in a wider account of democratic opportunity by refocusing attention from the contested periphery of the system of selection to its settled core. The present system measures merit through scores on paper-and-pencil tests. But this measure is fundamentally unfair. In the educational setting, it restricts opportunities for many poor and working-class Americans of all colors and genders who could otherwise obtain a better education. In the employment setting, it restricts access based on inadequate predictors of job performance. In short, it is neither fair nor functional in its distribution of opportunities for admission to higher education, entry-level hiring, and job promotion.

To be sure, the exclusion experienced by women and people of color is especially revealing of larger patterns. The race- and gender-based exclusions that are the target of current affirmative action policies remain the most visible examples of bias in ostensibly neutral selection processes. Objectionable in themselves, these exclusions also signal the inadequacy of traditional methods of selection for everyone, and the need to rethink how we allocate educational and employment opportunities. And that rethinking is crucial to our capacity to develop productive, fair, and efficient institutions that can meet the challenges of a rapidly changing and increasingly complex marketplace. By using the experience of those on the margin to rethink the whole, we may forge a new, progressive vision of cross-racial collaboration, functional diversity, and genuinely democratic opportunity.

AFFIRMATIVE ACTION NARRATIVES

Competing narratives drive the affirmative action debate. The stock story told by critics in the context of employment concerns the white civil servant—say, a police officer or firefighter—John Doe. (Similar stories abound in the educational setting.) Doe scores several points higher on the civil service exam and interview rating process, but loses out to a woman or person of color who did not score as high on those selection criteria.[1]

Doe and others in similar circumstances advance two basic claims: first, that they have more merit than beneficiaries of affirmative action; and second, that as a matter of fairness they are entitled to the position for which they applied. Consider these claims in turn.

The idea of merit can be interpreted in a variety of ways: for example, as a matter of desert (because they were next in line, based on established criteria of selection, they deserve the position), or as earned recognition ("when an individual has worked hard and succeeded, she deserves recognition, praise and/or reward"[2]). But, most fundamentally, arguments about merit are functional: a person merits a job if he or she has, to an especially high degree, the qualities needed to perform well in that job. Many critics of affirmative action equate merit, functionally understood, with a numerical ranking on standard paper-and-pencil tests. Those with higher scores are presumed to be most qualified, and therefore most deserving.

Fairness, like merit, is a concept with varying definitions. The stock story defines fairness formally. Fairness, it assumes, requires treating everyone the same: allowing everyone to enter the competition for a position, and evaluating each person's results the same way. If everyone takes the same test, and every applicant's test is evaluated in the same manner, then the assessment is fair. So affirmative action is unfair because it takes race and gender into account, and thus evaluates some test results differently. A crucial premise of this fairness challenge to affirmative action is the assumption that tests afford equal opportunity to demonstrate individual merit, and therefore are not biased.

Underlying the standard claims about merit and fairness, then, is the idea that we have an objective yardstick for measuring qualification. Institutions are assumed to know what they are looking for (to continue the yardstick analogy, length), how to measure it (yards, meters), how to replicate the measurement process (using the ruler), and how to rank people accordingly (by height). Both critics and proponents of affirmative action typically assume that objective tests for particular attributes of merit—perhaps supplemented by subjective methods such as unstructured interviews and reference checks—can be justified as predictive of performance, and as the most efficient method of selection.

MERIT, FAIRNESS, AND TESTOCRACY

The basic premise of the stock narrative is that the selection criteria and processes used to rank applicants for jobs and admission to schools are fair and valid tests of merit. This premise is flawed. The conventional system of selection does not give everyone an equal opportunity to compete. Not everyone who could do the job, or could bring new insights about how to do the job even better, is given an opportunity to perform or succeed. The yardstick metaphor simply does not withstand scrutiny.

Fictive Merit

For present purposes, we accept the idea that capacity to perform—functional merit—is a legitimate consideration in distributing jobs and educational opportunities. But we dispute the notion that merit is identical to performance on standardized tests. Such tests do not fulfill their stated function. They do not reliably identify those applicants who will succeed in college or later in life, nor do they consistently predict those who are most likely to perform well in the jobs they will occupy. Particularly when used alone or to rank-order candidates, timed paper-and-pencil tests screen out applicants who could nevertheless do the job.

Those who use standardized tests need to be able to identify and measure successful performance in the job or at school. In both contexts, however, those who use tests lack meaningful measures of successful performance. In the employment area, many employers have not attempted to correlate test performance with worker productivity or pay. In the educational context, researchers have attempted to correlate standardized tests with first-year performance in college or postgraduate education.[3] But this measure does not reflect successful overall academic achievement or performance in other areas valued by the educational institution.

Moreover, "successful performance" needs to be interpreted broadly. A study of three classes of Harvard alumni over three decades, for example, found a high correlation between "success"—defined by income, community involvement, and professional satisfaction—and two criteria that might not ordinarily be associated with Harvard freshmen: low SAT scores and a blue-collar background.[4] When asked what predicts *life success,* college admissions officers at elite universities report that, above a minimum level of competence, "initiative" or "drive" are the best predictors.[5]

By contrast, the conventional measures attempt to predict successful performance, narrowly defined, in the short run.

They focus on immediate success in school and a short time frame between taking the test and demonstrating success. Those who excel based on those short-term measures, however, may not in fact excel over the long run in areas that are equally or more important. For example, a study of graduates of the University of Michigan Law School found a negative relationship between high LSAT scores and subsequent community leadership or community service.[6]

Those with higher LSAT scores are less likely, as a general matter, to serve their community or do pro bono service as lawyers. In addition, the study found that admission indexes—including the LSAT—fail to correlate with other accomplishments after law school, including income levels and career satisfaction.

Standardized tests may thus compromise an institution's capacity to search for what it really values in selection. Privileging the aspects of performance measured by standardized tests may well screen out the contributions of people who would bring important and different skills to the workplace or educational institution. It may reward passive learning styles that mimic established strategies rather than creative, critical, or innovative thinking.

Finally, individuals often perform better in both the workplace and school when challenged by competing perspectives or when given the opportunity to develop in conjunction with the different approaches or skills of others.

The problem of using standardized tests to predict performance is particularly acute in the context of employment. Standardized tests may reward qualities such as willingness to guess, conformity, and docility. If they do, then test performance may not relate significantly to the capacity to function well in jobs that require creativity, judgment, and leadership. In a service economy, creativity and interpersonal skills are important, though hard to measure. In the stock scenario of civil service exams for police and fire departments, traits such as honesty, perseverance, courage, and ability to manage anger are left out. In other words, people who rely heavily on numbers to make employment decisions may be looking in the wrong place. While John Doe scored higher on the civil service exam, he may not perform better as a police officer.

Fictive Fairness

Scores on standardized tests are, then, inadequate measures of merit. But are the conventional methods of selecting candidates for high-stakes positions fair? The stock affirmative action narrative implicitly embraces the idea that fairness consists in sameness of treatment. But this conception of fairness assumes a level playing field—that if everyone plays by the same rules, the game does not favor or disadvantage anyone.

An alternative conception of fairness—we call it "fairness as equal access and opportunity"—rejects the automatic equation of sameness with fairness. It focuses on providing members of various races and genders with opportunities to demonstrate their capacities and recognizes that formal sameness can camouflage actual difference and apparently neutral screening devices can be exclusionary. The central idea is that the standards governing the process must not *arbitrarily advantage* members of one group over another. It is not "fair," in this sense, to use entry-level credentials that appear to treat everyone the same, but in effect deny women and people of color a genuine opportunity to demonstrate their capacities.

On this conception, the "testocracy" fails to provide a fair playing field for candidates. Many standardized tests assume that there is a single way to complete a job, and assess applicants solely on the basis of this uniform style. In this way, the testing process arbitrarily excludes individuals who may perform equally effectively, but with different approaches.

For example, in many police departments, strength, military experience, and speed weigh heavily in the decision to hire police officers. These characteristics relate to a particular mode of policing focusing on "command presence" and control through authority and force.[7]

If the job of policing is defined as subduing dangerous suspects, then it makes sense to favor the strongest, fastest, and most disciplined candidates. But not every situation calls for quick reaction time. Indeed, in some situations, responding quickly gets police officers and whole departments in trouble.

This speed-and-strength standard normalizes a particular type of officer: tough, brawny, and macho. But other modes of policing—dispute resolution, persuasion, counseling, and community involvement—are also critical, and sometimes superior, approaches to policing. One study of the Los Angeles Police Department, conducted in the wake of the Rodney King trials, recommended that the department increase the number of women on the police force as part of a strategy to reduce police brutality and improve community relations. The study found that women often display a more interactive and engaged approach to policing.[8]

Similarly, an informal survey of police work in some New York City Housing Authority projects found that many women housing authority officers, because they could not rely on their brawn to intimidate potential offenders, developed a mentoring style with young adolescent males.[9] The women, many of whom came from the community they were patrolling, increased public safety because they did not approach the young men in a confrontational way. Their authority was respected because they offered respect.

The retention and success of new entrants to institutions often depend on expanding measures of successful performance. But because conventional measures camouflage their bias, one-size-fits-all testocracies invite people to believe that they have earned their status because of a test score, and invite beneficiaries of affirmative action to believe exactly the opposite—that they did not earn their opportunity. By allowing partial and underinclusive selection standards to proceed without criticism, affirmative action perpetuates an asymmetrical approach to evaluation.

In addition to arbitrarily favoring certain standards of performance, conventional selection methods advantage candidates from higher socioeconomic backgrounds and disproportionately screen out women and people of color, as well as those in lower income brackets. When combined with other unstructured screening practices, such as personal connections and alumni preferences, standardized testing creates an arbitrary barrier for many otherwise-qualified candidates.

The evidence that the testocracy is skewed in favor of wealthy contestants is consistent and striking. Consider the linkage between test performance and parental income. Average family income rises with each hundred-point increase in SAT scores, except for the highest SAT category, where the number of cases is small. Within each racial and ethnic group, SAT scores increase with income.

Reliance on high school rank alone excludes fewer people from lower socioeconomic backgrounds. When the SAT is used in conjunction with high school rank to select college applicants, the number of applicants admitted from lower-income families decreases. This is because the SAT is more strongly correlated with every measure of socioeconomic background than is high school rank.[10]

Existing methods of selection, both objective and subjective, also exclude people based on their race and gender. For example, although women as a group perform worse than males perform on the SAT, they equal or outperform men in grade point average during the first year of college, the most common measure of successful performance. Similar patterns have been detected in the results of the ACT and other standardized college selection tests.[11]

Supplementing class rank with the SAT also decreases acceptances and enrollments of blacks.[12] Studies show that the group of black applicants rejected based on their SAT scores includes both those who would likely have failed and those who would likely have succeeded, and that these groups offset each other. Consequently, the rejection of more blacks as a result of using SAT scores "does not translate into improved admissions outcomes. The SAT does not improve colleges' ability to admit successful blacks and reject potentially unsuccessful ones."[13]

Thus, it is incontestable that the existing meritocracy disproportionately includes wealthy white men. Is this highly unequal outcome fair? Even if the "meritocracy" screens out women, people of color, and those of lower socioeconomic status, it could be argued that those screens are fair if they serve an important function. But the testocracy fails even on this measure; it does not reliably distinguish successful future performers from unsuccessful ones, even when supplemented by additional subjective criteria. Therefore, racial, gender, and socioeconomic exclusion cannot legitimately be justified in the name of a flawed system of selection.

A New Approach

We have seen how the stock affirmative action narrative normalizes and legitimates selection practices that are neither functional nor fair. Now it is time to use these criticisms as an occasion to move from affirmative action as an add-on to affirmative action as an occasion to rethink the organizing framework for selection generally.

Such rethinking should begin by reconsidering the connection between predetermined qualifications and future performance. The standard approach proceeds as if selection were a fine-tuned matching process that measures the capacity to perform according to some predetermined criteria of performance. This assumes that the capacity to perform—functional merit—exists in people apart from their opportunity to work on the job. It further assumes that institutions know in advance what they are looking for, and that these functions will remain constant across a wide range of work sites and over time.

But neither candidates nor positions remain fixed. Often people who have been given an opportunity to do a job perform well because they learn the job by doing it. Moreover, on-the-job learning has assumed even greater significance in the current economy, in which unstable markets, technological advances, and shorter product cycles have created pressures for businesses to increase the flexibility and problem-solving capacity of workers. Under these circumstances, access to on-the-job training opportunities will contribute to functional merit—the opportunity to perform will precede the capacity.

The concept of selection as a matching process also presumes that institutions have a clear idea of what they value, and of the relationship of particular jobs to their institutional goals. Even in a relatively stable economic and technological environment, institutions rarely attempt to articulate goals, much less develop a basis for measuring successful achievement of those goals. But without a definition of successful performance, it is difficult to develop fair and valid selection criteria and processes.

Defining successful performance has also become more complicated in the current economic and political environment. Traditional measures of success, such as short-term profitability, do not fully define success, and may in fact distort the capacity to evaluate and monitor employee performance. In addition, standards must increasingly change to adapt to technological developments and shifting consumer demand. Students of economic organization and human resources now emphasize the importance of developing complex, interactive, and holistic approaches to measuring both institutional and individual performance.[14] Conventional matching approaches to selection do not easily accommodate this move toward more dynamic and interrelated assessments of successful performance.

Current selection approaches also focus on the decontextualized individual, who is assumed to possess merit in the abstract and to demonstrate it through a test or interview.

Social science evidence shows that the testing environment can selectively depress the test performance of highly qualified individuals.[15] And individual performance does not take into account how an applicant functions as part of a group. Increasingly, work requires the capacity to interact effectively with others, and the demands of the economy are moving in the direction of more interactive, team-oriented production. The capacity to adapt to rapid changes in technology, shifts in consumer preferences, and fluid markets for goods requires greater collaboration at every level.[16] Paper-and-pencil tests do not measure or predict an individual's capacity for creativity and collaboration.

Assessment through opportunity to perform often works better than testing for performance. Various studies have shown that "experts often fail on 'formal' measures of their calculating or reasoning capacities but can be shown to exhibit precisely those same skills in the course of their ordinary work."[17] Those who assess individuals in situations that more closely resemble actual working conditions make better predictions about those individuals' ultimate performance. Particularly when those assessments are integrated into day-to-day work over a period of time, they have the potential to produce better information about workers and better workers.

Moreover, many of those who are given an opportunity to perform, even when their basic preparation is weaker, catch up if they are motivated to achieve. Indeed, a recent study of a twenty-five-year policy of open admissions at the City University of New York found that the school was one of the largest sources in the United States of undergraduate students going on to earn doctorates, even though many of its undergraduates come from relatively poor backgrounds and take twice as long to complete their bachelor's degree.[18]

RECLAIMING MERIT AND FAIRNESS

Critics of affirmative action defend prevailing selection practices in the name of meritocracy and democracy. We have argued that those practices put democratic opportunity fundamentally at risk. Even when they are modified by a commitment to affirmative action, current modes of selection jeopardize democratic values of inclusiveness (no one is arbitrarily shut out or excluded), transparency (the processes employed are open and are functionally linked to the public character or public mission of the institution), and accountability (the choice of beneficiaries is directly linked to a public good). The failure of existing practice to achieve inclusiveness is perhaps the most telling. Although some people will lose as a result of any sorting and ranking, a democratic system needs to give those losers a sense of hope in the future, not divide us into classes of permanent losers and permanent winners. But that is precisely what happens when we make opportunity dependent on past success.

How, then, can we develop a model of selection that expresses a more inclusive, transparent, and accountable vision of democratic opportunity—an approach to selection that will benefit everyone, and advance racial and gender justice?

An Emerging Model

Because of the importance in a democracy of ensuring opportunities to perform, we can start by shifting the model of selection from prediction to performance. This model builds on the insight that the opportunity to participate helps to create the capacity to perform, and that actual performance offers the best evidence of capacity to perform. So instead of making opportunity depend on a strong prior showing of qualification, we should expand opportunities as a way of building the relevant qualifications.

To follow this model, organizations need to build assessment into their activities, integrate considerations of inclusion and diversity into the process of selection, and develop mechanisms of evaluation that are accountable to those considerations. The result would be a dynamic process of selection, with feedback integrated into productivity. At the level of individual performance assessment, it would mean less reliance on one-shot predictive tests and more on performance-based evaluation.

One fundamental change resulting from our framework would be a shift away from reliance on tests as a means of distinguishing among candidates. Tests would be limited to screening out individuals who could not learn to perform competently with adequate training and mentoring, or be simply discontinued as a part of the selection process. Of course, decreasing reliance on tests to rank candidates would create the need to develop other ways of distinguishing among applicants. There is no single, uniform solution to this problem. One approach would be a lottery system that would distribute opportunity to participate among relatively indistinguishable candidates by chance. Concerns about a lottery's insensitivity to particular institutional needs or values could be addressed by increasing the selection prospects of applicants with skills, abilities, or backgrounds that are particularly valued by the institution. A weighted lottery may be the fairest and most functional approach for some institutions. Particularly in the education arena, where opportunity lies at the core of the institution's mission, a lottery may be an important advance. Above that test-determined floor, applicants could be chosen by several alternatives, including portfolio-based assessment or a more structured and participatory decision-making process.[19]

A more institutionally grounded approach might work in noneducational contexts. In some jobs, for example, decision makers would assume responsibility for constructing a dynamic and interactive process of selection that is integrated into the day-to-day functioning of the organization. Recent developments in the assessment area, such as portfolio-based and authentic assessment, move in this direction. These might build on the tradition and virtues of apprenticeship, and indeed might "more closely resemble traditional apprenticeship measures than formal testing."[20] They would build from and acknowledge the effects of context on performance and the importance of measuring performance in relation to context.

To take the next step in developing an experience-based approach to opportunity and assessment, it would be necessary to consider the needs, interests, and possibilities of the particular institutional setting. The central challenge is to develop systems of accountable decision making that minimize the expression of bias and structure judgment around identified, although not static, norms. For each assessment, decision makers would articulate criteria of successful performance, document activities and tasks relevant to the judgment, assess candidates in relation to those criteria, and offer sufficient information about the candidates' performance to enable others to exercise independent judgment.

For this model to work, institutions would also need to change the relationship between race, gender, and other categories of exclusion to the overall decision-making process. Institutions would continue to assess the impact of various selection processes on traditionally excluded groups. But institutions would use that information in different ways. Rather than operating as an add-on, after-the-fact response to failures of the overall process, race and gender would serve as both a signal of organizational failure and a catalyst of organizational innovation. We will return to this issue later, but let's first try to imagine what this more integrated approach would look like.

*   *   *

Consider the case of Bernice, now the general counsel of a major financial institution. Initially, she was hired as local general counsel to a bank, after having previously been partner in a prestigious law firm. (She left the firm after reaching the glass ceiling, unable to bring in enough new clients to progress further.)

Bernice ultimately became general counsel to a major national corporation that previously had no women in high-level management positions. Her promotion resulted from the opportunities presented in an interactive and extended selection process. Her local bank merged with a larger company. In part to create the appearance of including women, she was permitted to compete for the job of general counsel for the new entity. Three lawyers shared the position for nine months. She initially did not view herself as in the running for the final cut.

During this time period, Bernice had a series of contacts with high-level corporate officials, contacts she never would have had without this probationary team approach. As it turned out, Bernice was able to deal unusually well with a series of crises. If standard criteria, such as recommendations and interpersonal contacts, had been used to select a candidate, it is doubtful Bernice would have been picked. But teamwork, decentralized management, and collaborative and flexible working relationships allowed her to develop the contacts and experiences that trained her. The opportunity to interact over a period of time allowed her to demonstrate her strengths to those who made promotion decisions. Bernice did not know she had those strengths until she took the job.[21]

Now, as general counsel, she is positioned to expand opportunities for women, and corporate culture in general. She can structure the same kind of collaborative decision making in selection that provided her the opportunity to work her way into the job. She determines who is promoted within the legal department, and who is hired as outside counsel. She is also in a position to influence how women are assessed as managers within the company.

This story illustrates the potential for integrating concerns about diversity into the process of recruitment and selection. It also shows the value of using performance to assess performance. At the core of this integrative move is a functional theory of diversity animated both by principles of justice and fairness (the inclusion of marginalized groups and the minimization of bias) and by strategic concerns (improving productivity). It is crucial to this integration that decision makers and advocates understand and embrace a conception of diversity that comprises normative and instrumental elements. In public discourse, diversity has become a catchall phrase or cliché used to substitute for a variety of goals, or a numerical concept that is equated with proportional representation.[22] Too often, the different strands of diversity remain separate, with those concerned about justice emphasizing racial and gender diversity as a project of remediation, and those concerned about productivity emphasizing differences in background and skills. Without an articulated theory that links diversity to the goals of particular enterprises and to the project of racial justice, public discussion and public policy making around race and gender issues is more complicated.

Selection and Productivity

One argument for more closely integrating selection and performance is that doing so has the potential to improve institutions' capacity to select productive workers, pursue innovative performance, and adapt quickly to the demands of a changing economic environment. The conventional top-down approach short-circuits the capacity of selection to serve as a mechanism for feedback about an institution's performance and its need to adapt to changing conditions. It also keeps institutions from developing more responsive, integrated, and dynamically efficient selection processes.

Instead of relying on standardized tests, the system of performance-based selection would focus decision makers' attention on creating suitable scenarios for making informed judgments about performance. This would improve the capacity of institutions to find people who are creative, adaptive, reliable, and committed, rather than just good test takers. In some instances, these structured opportunities could directly contribute to the productivity of the organization.

A more interactive process of selection also provides an

ongoing opportunity to assess and monitor organizational performance and to perceive and react to the changing character and needs of clients and employees. It provides information learned through the process of selection to the rest of the organization. In the process of redefining the standards for recruitment, the organization also redefines how those already in the institution should function. Selection operates at the boundaries of the organization. It exposes decision makers to the environment they operate in, provides access to information about the world in which the organization operates, and forces choices about its relationship with that environment. The process of defining the standards for positions also reflects and reinscribes the organization's priorities and direction. Emphasizing one set of skills over another in the selection process communicates to employees and students how the organization defines good work. Thus, the selection process provides the opportunity and challenge of continually redefining standards in relation to stakeholders, both inside and outside of the organization.

The Benefits of Diversity

More open-ended processes of selection also embrace and harness difference. And the resulting diversity—in particular, an interactive dynamic among individuals with different vantage points, skills, or values—appears to help generate creative solutions to problems.

Studies have shown that work-team heterogeneity promotes more critical strategic analysis, creativity, innovation,
and high-quality decisions. Analyses of group decision
making suggest that participation of groups with different
prior beliefs or predispositions in decision making improves
the quality of the decision for everyone. Studies of jury de-
liberations support the contention that diversity of participants contributes to improved deliberation. A jury con-
sisting of people from diverse backgrounds has more
accurate recall and "more nuanced understanding of the behavior of the parties than [a more homogeneous jury]."[23]

Diversity in culture, style, and background also enhan-
ces the knowledge base and repertoire of skills and responses available to a particular group or institution, which
can enhance institutions' capacity to perform and innovate.
Again, the example of the Los Angeles Police Department
illustrates this theory. The benefits of racial and gender diversity may be most obvious in the educational and human
services areas, where customers, clients, and perspectives
may themselves be identified by race and gender.

Racial and cultural diversity in a workforce can also provide opportunities for companies marketing products that
serve racially and culturally diverse client groups. As David
Thomas and Robin Ely have documented, customers and
clients from different racial, ethnic, and cultural communities constitute distinctive market niches that companies
have sought to address by diversifying their workforces.

Inside an organization, the experience of those who have

been excluded or marginalized often signals more general or systemic problems that affect a much larger group and may hurt the organization's overall productivity. Race and gender complaints may be symptomatic of more general management problems, such as poor organization or arbitrary treatment of workers. For example, recent studies documenting that many women find law school silencing and exclusionary reveal patterns of problems that many men experience as well.[24]

Similarly, sexual harassment of graduate students sometimes reveals a more general institutional inadequacy that would otherwise remain hidden. Faculty and students frequently lack shared understandings about fair, respectful, nonexploitative supervisory relationships between students and their faculty advisors. Addressing sexual harassment—a problem ordinarily associated with women—can prompt a conversation on ways to promote productive and successful working relationships in general.

These observations answer a large question about the status of affirmative action in the performance-based model: Once we use the lens of the margins to rethink the whole, why do group status and performance continue to be crucial in assessing the adequacy of selection criteria? If we are successful in transforming the discourse and practice of merit and selection for everyone, why are race, gender, and other categories of exclusion still relevant to the discussion?

In responding to these questions, we take the world as it

currently exists. The workforce is becoming increasingly diverse: almost two thirds of entrants to the civilian workforce in the period between 1992 and 2005 are projected to be women and racial minorities. Women and people of color have long been excluded and marginalized, and continue to experience exclusion in many institutional settings. Race continues to be a divisive issue for many Americans, one that prompts skepticism and mistrust. Our continued focus on race and gender moves forward from the current legal and organizational landscape. In many institutions, particularly those that are private and nonunion, categories such as race and gender offer the only avenue for challenging decisions and practices.

Under these conditions, race- and gender-based inquiries continue to form the cornerstone of an integrated approach to a progressive economic agenda. Many members of marginalized groups predicate their willingness to participate in collaborative conversation on the majority's recognition of the ongoing significance of group-based exclusion. For members of historically excluded groups, a meaningful program of inclusion is a prerequisite to participating in ventures that benefit the whole community. Affirmative action has become a symbol of society's recognition of its responsibility for its history of legal disenfranchisement, and of the equal citizenship and respect of those who have historically been excluded. History shapes the perception and experience of those who have experienced formal exclusion, and this historic pattern of racial inequality will continue to be experienced unless it is affirmatively acknowledged and altered.

Without the cooperation of those concerned with race and gender justice in building this new progressive agenda, the dialogue will continue to be polarized, divisive, and adversarial. Unless we can build the concerns of racial and gender inclusion into the process of collaboration, these issues will continue to be addressed in settings that undermine the capacity of institutions to adapt to changing conditions.

In addition, research consistently shows that ignoring patterns of racial and gender exclusion causes these patterns to recur. A proven method of minimizing the expression of bias in decision making consists of reminding decision makers of the risk of bias or exclusion and requiring them to be fair and unbiased. Unless we continue to pay attention to the impact of our decisions on members of groups that are the target of subtle bias and exclusion, those group members will continue to be marginalized.

Fairness

Using the margins to rethink the whole—by using performance to develop opportunity—will help with fairness as well as functionality. The functional approach to selection reduces the importance of criteria that have excluded women and people of color and favored wealthier applicants. It enables previously excluded people to "show their stuff." Moreover, by rethinking the standards of selection for everyone, this approach destabilizes the idea that the existing meritocracy is fair. Embedding the role of diversity enables other people to see how benefiting women and people of color benefits them. In addition, the functional approach has the potential to create a participatory and accountable selection process, which can enhance individuals' autonomy and institutions' legitimacy.

Finally, conditions for sustained contact, genuine collaboration, and fair assessment provide outsiders with a meaningful opportunity to learn, perform, and succeed. Studies of multiracial teamwork suggest that the opportunity to work as relative coequals in interdependent, cooperative teams may also reduce bias.[25] Indeed, carefully structured, accountable, and participatory work groups may replicate the conditions most likely to reduce bias and permit genuine participation by women and people of color.

To be sure, these more interactive and informal forms of selection and management rely explicitly on discretion and subjectivity. Preconceptions and biases will likely affect evaluations of performance in ways that often exclude women and people of color. And unstructured discretion exercised without accountability or participation by diverse decision makers will likely reproduce biased and exclusionary results. But these biases have not been eliminated by formal selection practices and paper-and-pencil tests. More important, the model of formal fairness that is outcome-driven, rule-bound, and centralized will not reach many of the places where women and people of color seek to enter.[26] If the economy is moving in the direction of creating and restructuring work along more team-oriented, participatory lines, we need approaches to selection and performance that permit women and people of color to participate fairly and to succeed in this changing environment. Otherwise, women and people of color will remain on the margins of the new economy. Moreover, as business entities become more fluid and rely more on subcontracting and temporary work, we must devise new and more interactive strategies for inclusion and empowerment that embrace a workforce existing in the margins of traditional legal categories. The exercise of discretion cannot and should not be eliminated. Instead, discretionary decision making must become the subject and site of participation, accountability, and creative problem solving.

A Democratic Imperative

Access to work and education is a fundamental attribute of modern citizenship. Work provides an identity that is valued by others. Work organizes and shapes the citizen's sense of self. Virtually every aspect of citizenship is channeled through participation in the workplace. For most people, medical care, pensions, and social insurance are linked to workplace participation. In these ways, work has become a proxy for citizenship.

Increasingly, the opportunity to work in a noncontingent, full-time position that provides these benefits of citizenship depends on access to higher education. People who do not have that access do not get jobs, and thus cannot participate in the responsibilities and benefits of citizenship. Moreover, those without the benefits of higher education increasingly work in shifting, temporary, and task-centered jobs. Such individuals may fail to develop a sense of personal worth, institutional or communal loyalty, or positive agency, all attributes essential to functioning as citizens.

In addition, voting—the process that has traditionally served to permit participation and influence public decision making—does not afford individuals the capacity to deliberate and exercise much influence over the conditions of day-to-day life. Without the opportunity to participate in intermediate institutions, such as places of work and schools, many citizens have no sense that their voices are being heard.[27]

If, as we believe, work and education are basic components of citizenship, screens or barriers to participation should be drawn in the least exclusive manner consistent with the institution's mission. Access and opportunity to participate is critical to equipping citizens to fulfill their responsibilities, to respecting their status and autonomy as individuals, and to legitimating society's decisions as reflecting the participation of the community. People who feel they have a voice in the decision-making process are more likely to accept the ultimate decision as legitimate, even if it is different from the one they initially supported.

Through the first two centuries of our nation's history, restrictions on voting based on race, gender, and wealth were gradually lifted "only after wide public debate" about "the very nature of the type of society in which Americans wished to live."[28] These barriers were invalidated because they came to be seen as unduly burdening access to this fundamental aspect of citizenship. Courts also recognized that these burdens, through the exercise of selective discretion by local officials, fell disproportionately on disempowered groups such as African Americans.[29]

We believe a national debate on the terms of participation in equivalent forms of citizenship is long overdue. Just as "history has seen a continuing expansion of the scope of the right of suffrage in this country,"[30] so we would argue that twenty-first-century democracy will depend on a commensurate expansion of the scope of access to higher education and opportunities for on-the-job training. Even if there are justifications for requirements relating to the capacity to exercise citizenship responsibilities effectively, these requirements must be drawn in the most narrow way possible because of the importance of assuring democratic access and legitimacy in the distribution of citizenship opportunities and responsibilities. A performance-based framework of selection is the equivalent, in employment and education, to the elimination of poll taxes and restrictive registration laws in the arena of voting.

We seek to open up a conversation about issues that many

people treat as resolved. Our institutions do not currently function as fair and functional meritocracies. Only by rethinking our assumptions about the current system and future possibilities can we move toward the ideals that so many Americans share. This enterprise offers the possibility of bringing together many who are adversaries in the current affirmative action debate but share an interest in forging fairer, more inclusive, and more democratic institutions. It reconnects affirmative action to the innovative ideal. In this way, affirmative action can reclaim the historic relationship between racial justice and the revitalization of institutions to the benefit of everyone.

2

MENDING AFFIRMATIVE ACTION

The purpose of affirmative action is to break down the wall of occupational segregation that excluded racial minorities and women from entire occupational sectors throughout American history. Whatever else one might want to say about affirmative action, it has achieved its policy objective: substantial desegregation of the American workplace, for women and minorities alike. This is true not only in the professions and in corporate management, but also in major blue-collar industries and in the public sector where nearly one out of every three black workers is employed. If logic and principle had prevailed, we would now be exploring ways to expand affirmative action to industries and job sectors that have been immune to change.

The problem is that "for more than two decades, affirmative action has been under sustained assault," as Sturm and Guinier write in their opening sentence. Though they do not say so explicitly, they seem resigned to the fact that the Supreme Court, which has already eviscerated affirmative action through a series of decisions, is now poised to deliver the coup de grâce. Against this background, Sturm and Guinier declare that "it is time to shift the terrain of debate." The entire thrust of their argument is to explore alternatives to affirmative action that will broaden access of minorities and women to jobs and universities.

At first blush, this strategy may appear to be a sensible concession to political reality. However, two troubling questions arise. First, are Sturm and Guinier capitulating to the anti–affirmative action backlash and prematurely throwing in the towel for the sake of an illusory consensus? Second, would their proposed reforms of the selection process, even if enacted, provide the access to jobs and opportunities that are today secured by affirmative action?

The logic of Sturm and Guinier's brief can be stated as follows:

1. Affirmative action is assailed by critics as violating cherished principles of "merit."

2. On closer examination, the "testocracy" that is used to assess merit is neither fair nor functional.

3. Therefore—alas, here the syllogism runs into trouble. Sturm and Guinier could have concluded that the case against affirmative action is specious and therefore affirmative action should be upheld. As the saying goes, "if it ain't broke, don't fix it."

Instead Sturm and Guinier make a case for overhauling the selection process that evaluates candidates for jobs and college admissions. To be sure, there are compelling arguments for abandoning standardized tests that favor privileged groups who, aside from the advantages that derive from better schooling, have the resources to pay for expensive prep courses. Sturm and Guinier also make a compelling case that it would be fairer and more productive to judge applicants on the basis of performance criteria, rather than scores on "paper-and-pencil" tests. The problem, though, is that they implicitly advocate these reforms as a surrogate for affirmative action policy. They may tell themselves that they are driven by realpolitik, but they end up acquiescing to the reversal of hard-won gains and falling back on reforms that are unlikely to be enacted in the foreseeable future. Their ideological enemies will revel in this retreat to a second line of defense by two law professors who are identified with the cause of affirmative action. Nor will Sturm and Guinier get the concessions they are bargaining for. Is this not the lesson of Bill Clinton's ill-fated proposal to "end welfare as we know it"?

What evidence is there that overhauling the selection criteria would open up avenues for women and minorities? In most large-scale organizations—corporations and universities alike—employees are routinely evaluated by superiors on an array of performance criteria. Is so-and-so a "team player"? Does she do her job well? Does he have good communication skills? Does she make the tough decisions? Does he demonstrate leadership? Such judgments are easily tainted by personal prejudices, especially when the people doing the evaluations are white and male and the people being evaluated belong to stigmatized groups. Indeed, studies have consistently found that performance appraisal ratings of women and people of color are prone to bias.

A second problem with the "performance-based model" advocated by Sturm and Guinier is that the benefits would be diffused to many groups, and could easily miss African Americans, who were the original targets of affirmative action policy. Besides, how do people demonstrate "performance" when they cannot get their foot in the door?

Finally, Sturm and Guinier place emphasis on jobs "where customers, clients, and perspectives may themselves be identified by race and gender." Granted, corporations need black managers to interface with the black consumer market, and police departments need women to deal with domestic violence. But women and minorities deserve equal access to *all* jobs in the workforce. Though Sturm and Guinier endorse this principle, their proposal runs the risk of typing jobs by gender and race, thereby validating the patterns of internal segregation that exist within many job structures.

The lesson of history is that the only mechanism that has ever worked to counteract occupational segregation is affirmative action, and that even good-faith efforts were ineffectual until they were backed up with specific goals and timetables. Too much is at stake to retreat to a second line of defense, especially one so fraught with difficulty. The crusade against affirmative action may well be on the verge of achieving its nefarious objective. But this is all the more reason to remain steadfast in defense of a policy that has not only advanced the cause of justice for women and minorities, but in doing so, has enhanced American democracy. Instead of venturing into the realm of personnel relations and testing, it would have been far better had Sturm and Guinier used their talents as legal scholars to plead the case for affirmative action. As we know it.

LOVE'S LABOR LOST? WHY RACIAL FAIRNESS IS A THREAT TO MANY WHITE AMERICANS

DERRICK BELL

I wholeheartedly agree with Susan Sturm and Lani Guinier's well-documented position asserting that basing merit on the results of standardized paper-and-pencil tests is both inaccurate and unfair. The data they cite is eye-opening. Their arguments for reform are compelling. And, because civil rights proponents often view policy flexibility as a form of moral deficiency, I welcome the authors' urging affirmative action advocates to move beyond unbending support for racial preference programs as the only workable remedy to counter decades of intentional discrimination.

As presently administered, the scores on standardized tests more accurately measure the economic status of the test takers than they measure their potential for success in school or on the job. They reward as worthy of merit the already well-off while serving as one more barrier to disadvantaged test takers, white as well as black. Unintentionally, to be sure, but no less certainly, affirmative action policies have bestowed undeserved legitimacy on tests and other generally used selection criteria that, in fact, are deeply flawed.

Unfortunately, in this country, when the topic for discussion involves race, myth and stereotype easily supplant accuracy, logic, and even common sense. Assume, to make my point, that all opponents of affirmative action read and considered the Sturm-Guinier test-taking reforms and then were asked to vote for or against these new selection methods. My experience indicates that to the extent that the reforms were viewed as helpful to minorities, despite their capacity to benefit whites as well, they would be rejected as just a jazzed-up version of affirmative action.

The problem is not with the authors' work. I find the Sturm-Guinier suggestions for abandoning standardized testing in favor of more accurate measures worthy of adoption. Their review of the seldom seen statistics on just how poorly standardized tests measure merit or predict success are astounding to even this writer, long suspicious of the value of such tests. And yet, like so many civil rights initiatives that not only have the potential but actually help more whites than blacks, the designation of the Sturm-Guinier suggestions as a policy with civil rights implications renders it immediately suspect, a political form of "love's labor lost." And, I think I know why.

* * *

Early in my law-teaching career that followed a decade of work as a civil rights litigator and administrator, I devised a formula that might help the students in my Racism and the Law course understand the societal physics of race in America: (1) when an issue places in conflict racist policy and racial justice, racism wins every time; and (2) when an issue is viewed as pitting self-interest for whites against the perpetuation of racism, justice for blacks is the nominal outcome.

Some of my students were appalled at my seeming cynicism, but the formula accurately tracks the approach to every racial policy decision in the nation's history. No matter how grievous the racial injustice, no action is taken until policy makers comprehend that it will advantage the country to at least acknowledge the injustices and make symbolic moves to remedy them.

Consider how the formula worked when applied to affirmative action. Even a dozen years after the Supreme Court's 1954 decision holding racial segregation unconstitutional as maintained by governmental entities, the hiring and placement of blacks and other people of color had hardly moved beyond the realm of tokenism. Despite the mandates of law and basic fairness, most corporations, government agencies, and educational institutions retained their mostly white, male character. The issue was one between maintaining racially discriminatory personnel practices or changing those policies so as to provide justice for blacks. Racism won.

These views began to change after the Los Angeles riots of 1966, and they received close scrutiny in the wake of the dozens of urban rebellions following Dr. Martin Luther King Jr.'s assassination in 1968. Suddenly, their all-white status made institutions uncomfortable. Fear compelled policy makers to "do something." For the next several years, there was a discernible effort to bring more women and minorities into the workforce, the government agencies, even college faculties. Part 2 of the formula kicked in. Now, it was a matter of self-interest versus racism, and the result, at least for a while, was justice for blacks.

Civil rights gains, though, are never vested or permanent. With the fear generated by race riots diminished, the resistance to racial justice that had been simmering below the surface during the aftermath of the riots returned with a vengeance. Part 1 regained its dominant position. Opponents began winning cases challenging affirmative action policies. Politicians, like Jesse Helms, defeated more able black candidates like Charlotte Mayor and Harvey Gantt, by linking them with affirmative action. Helms did it with the now famous television commercial in which a pair of white hands are shown tearing up a rejection slip while the voice-over announces that the job went to a less-qualified minority.

Professors Sturm and Guinier dismiss such anti–affirmative action scenarios as "stock stories." They might with no greater success attempt to dismiss Christianity by claiming the virgin birth is a stock story. For many whites, affirmative action is seen as a program for blacks and thus a threat to whites. No matter that white women have been the chief beneficiaries of these programs. Opponents seldom mention white women in their attacks. They ignore as well the fact that affirmative action policies require the advertising of thousands of positions enabling white men to learn of and apply for jobs that under the old-boy network would have been filled without their ever hearing about them.

What is the source of this hostility on the part of poor and middle-class whites to policies that actually help them? The answer is one racial reformers must consider even though the barriers prove insurmountable.

In America, where property is a measure of worth, many whites—with relatively little property of a traditional kind, money, securities, land—view their whiteness as a property right. A number of scholars are now writing about this phenomenon.[1] One of them, Professor Cheryl Harris, in "A Property in Whiteness," a frequently quoted *Harvard Law Review* article, asserts: "The valorization of whiteness as treasured property takes place in a society structured on racial caste. In ways so embedded that it is rarely apparent, the set of assumptions, privileges, and benefits that accompany the status of being white have become a valuable asset that whites sought to protect. . . . Whites have come to expect and rely on these benefits, and over time these expectations have been affirmed, legitimated, and protected in law."[2]

Professor Harris explains: "The wages of whiteness are available to all whites regardless of class position, even to those whites who are without power, money, or influence. Whiteness, the characteristic that distinguishes them from Blacks, serves as compensation even to those who lack material wealth. It is the relative political advantage extended to whites, rather than actual economic gains, that are crucial to white workers."[3]

She explains the opposition by so many whites to civil rights policies including affirmative action by suggesting that political advantage over blacks requires that whites not identify with blacks even on matters that transcend skin color. To give continued meaning to their whiteness, whites must identify with whites at the top of the economic pile, not with blacks with whom—save color—they have so much in common. This identification based on whiteness was obviously at work in the 2000 presidential elections, causing a great many whites to vote the Republican ticket despite that party's advocacy of many policies that would further enrich the wealthy at the expense of the middle-class to which they belonged.

Sturm and Guinier call for a national debate intended to spotlight the benefits of performance-based selection systems and their potential for bringing greater efficiency as well as fairness into the job market. They hope to allay the fears and hostility of those who opposed affirmative action in its traditional forms by showing that their new selection policies will enable opponents to recognize that they resemble part 2 (self-interest) rather than part 1 (racism) of my formula. I join them in this hope while cautioning that getting whites to see what is truly in their interests in racial matters is a very tough, and if history is any indication may prove an impossible, task.

VYGOTSKY TO THE RESCUE!

HOWARD GARDNER

About a decade ago, I was approached by a group of law school admissions directors. They asked whether I, as a cognitive psychologist interested in new forms of assessment, could help to redesign the law school aptitude test. I asked one question, which effectively terminated the mission of these good people. The question: "Do you want to change law school?"

Buried in this question are two assumptions that dominate assessment in this country at this time. We might call the first the "end state" assumption. It is assumed that the capacities purportedly measured by an instrument like the LSAT are critical for successful execution of an ultimate goal or "end state." I am not an expert on law school, but I suspect that the LSAT is much better as a predictor of who will make law review or become a good professor of law than as a predictor of who will be a good litigator or good arbitrator, or even who will make the most money. Law school, however, remains the domain of law professors, so we could reasonably expect that they would favor instruments that allow them to replicate themselves.

The second assumption could be termed the "trait" assumption. Drawing on a long (but perhaps prejudicial) tradition in Anglo-American thought, such instruments assume that individuals possess (or fail to possess) certain "traits," and that not much can be done about this state of affairs. Some individuals have the "it" required to be an effective law student and lawyer; the earlier and more unequivocally we can ascertain who has "it," the better for all concerned.

I join Susan Sturm and Lani Guinier in questioning both of these assumptions. I suspect that there are many legal "end states" and that present instruments are heavily skewed toward just a few of the more readily measurable ones. In addition, I doubt that "lawyerness" (whatever it is or isn't) is something that individuals possess (or fail to possess) to a certain degree. I think it far more likely that many individuals have the potential to be lawyers of quality and—key point—that much more powerful ways could be developed to ascertain that potential.

Until now, I have limited my remarks to the practice of law. I must stress, therefore, that these same assumptions about assessment dominate every sphere of educational and professional life. From admission to an independent school to admission to the bar, from the police force to the teaching force, we assume too blithely that we know the relation between the "entry point" and the "end state." Moreover, we assume too blithely the existence of traits or aptitudes that individuals either possess or lack. Indeed, it was less than a decade ago that the College Board reluctantly removed the word *aptitude* from the SAT—while keeping largely unchanged the assumptions built into its instruments.

Without explicitly noting it, Sturm and Guinier have built their case on a concept developed seventy-five years ago by a brilliant Russian psychologist named Lev Semonovich Vygotsky. Vygotsky speculated about two individuals—let's call them Boris and Mikhail—who received the same score on some task, say, a set of items on an intelligence test. The average observer would assume that these individuals had the same ability, trait, aptitude, or skill. Vygotsky had the clever idea of providing the same amount of training or tutelage to both of these individuals—to use a current word of art, he provided them both with considerable "scaffolding." If both individuals' scores remained the same at the end of this period, or if both improved by the same amount, we could reasonably infer that they had similar ability.

Suppose, however, that Boris's score went up just a tad while Mikhail's score improved by 25 percent. Moreover, a few weeks later, Boris's score remained steady, while Mikhail's had continued to rise. We should properly infer that there is an important difference between the two lads: that Mikhail has a greater potential to learn and would presumably benefit more from an enriched educational environment. Vygotsky labeled his concept "the zone of proximal development"; application of this concept allows one to ascertain amount of improvement—particularly lasting improvement—under conditions of moderate help.

I read Sturm and Guinier as witting or unwitting Vygotskians. They are arguing that we should identify skills and capacities that are important and determine the extent to which individuals exposed to an appropriately rich environment can pick up or amplify these skills and capacities. To put it in vernacular terms: they seek to import the mind-set of "on-the-job training" to the terrain of "assessing potential." To put it in terms of the assumptions I introduced above: Sturm and Guinier would like us to discard the notion that there is a pure trait that is presumed to be a phenotype of future success in a domain. Instead, they urge us to place a candidate in an environment in which experts are exhibiting requisite skills and capacities, and then determine the extent to which, and the speed with which, the candidate can acquire these skills and capacities. Instead of a presumed distant end state, we provide actual "living" instances of the end state. And instead of a mysterious inborn "trait," we look for individuals who can begin to exhibit the desired skills and behaviors as the result of limited but targeted immersion in the appropriate environment.

The critiques of standardized tests offered by Sturm and Guinier are familiar ones. Indeed, the journalist Walter Lippmann offered most of them in the 1920s. Various attempts have been made to overthrow this orthodoxy, from logical arguments to legal challenges to blatant ridicule—some thirty years ago, psychologists developed the "Chitlin test" of intellectual competence, which (as the name implies) presupposed cultural literacy in the African American world.

Observers sympathetic to the critiques must ask why standardized tests remain so robust, particularly in this country. Sturm and Guinier identify some of the reasons. To them, I would add two more: the lack of an alternative way of thinking about assessment and the paucity of alternative instruments or methods.

In their essay, Sturm and Guinier contribute chiefly to our thinking about new ways of assessing. I broadly endorse their stress on performance of relevant tasks rather than on measurement of hypothesized abilities or traits, and I think that the Vygotskian analysis can provide intellectual support for this position. In the absence of demonstrated alternatives, though, standardized tests (as we have grown to love or hate them) will continue to hold sway.

Let me offer two modest proposals that might allow one to explore the applicability of their ideas—for the sake of argument, in the case of prospective law students. The first involves a summer or term-long internship. Interested candidates could agree to work in a law office as volunteers or for a modest stipend. They would be involved immediately in tasks for which they do not require special training, but which could test their capacity to "pick up" needed understandings. Those who catch on most successfully to relevant legal roles (including the social, creative, and flexible skills emphasized by Sturm and Guinier) would earn special credits toward admission to law school. Of course, we would have to ascertain whether students thus admitted could succeed in (standard or revised) law school and go on to practice law successfully thereafter.

The continuing improvement of computer software suggests a second approach. One could create simulations of skills and proficiencies important for success in the study and actual practice of law. Some law schools now include a special course called "lawyering," which seeks to cultivate a wide gamut of skills relevant to successful legal practice. The simulations could be drawn from the lawyering curriculum. Vygotsky-style, they could provide varying degrees of scaffolding. Those students who perform well in such simulations, and who continue to improve over successive trials, would earn similar credits toward admission. Again, it would be necessary to determine whether success in such simulated environments predicts success in law school and in the law office.

Until now, we have skewed education everywhere toward "uniform" approaches—*one* way of teaching, *one* way of assessment, *one* standard of success. Reflective practitioners know, however, that this is at best an oversimplification and perhaps an ultimate disservice to candidates, to the profession, to the larger society. Sturm and Guinier have put forth an appealing alternative vision. Only a powerful sense of purpose, artful technology, and support to carry out needed experiments can reveal whether this alternative vision is viable.

THE PROMISE OF DIVERSITY

MARY C. WATERS AND CAROLYN BOYES-WATSON

Sturm and Guinier argue that affirmative action merely nibbles at the margins of inherently unfair structures of opportunity because the primary methods for assessing applicants for admission to higher education, entry-level jobs, and promotion are neither functional nor fair. As prediction mechanisms, standardized tests are pretty ineffective in reading the future performance of prospective students or employees. And, of course, they tell us nothing about drive, motivation, or the values an individual brings to his or her career and future contribution to society. As methods for ensuring fairness, standardized tests behave even worse: test scores are highly correlated with socioeconomic status and reflect the cumulative advantages of class rather than the inherent abilities of the candidate. As an alternative to testing, Sturm and Guinier propose a daring shift in our approach to selection: right now we are busy trying to assess the talents of individuals *before* they begin school or begin a job. But what if we were to simply reverse the order? Suppose we distribute the *opportunity* to perform through more direct and fair methods and determine *merit* of the candidates based on the quality of their actual performance in school or on the job itself?

We think this is a novel and potentially exciting way to widen the structure of opportunity. And for the most part, we agree with the authors' critique of standardized testing. But does the robust critique of standardized testing offered by Sturm and Guinier also spell doom for the policy of affirmative action? Are these two issues necessarily joined at the hip? Or is it possible to decouple the issues—to reject standardized testing while recognizing the need for affirmative action policies?

We think it is wise to separate these two issues from one another. We doubt that the alternative vision proposed by the authors would, on its own, produce fair outcomes and create diversity in schools and workplaces. On the contrary, we believe that, in the absence of the legal framework of affirmative action, the Sturm and Guinier approach to selection would have a regressive impact on the very goals they aspire to achieve.

The argument that much standardized testing is of questionable value in predicting future success, and largely reflects the past cultural and economic advantages of the test taker, is hardly new. But with the testing mania currently sweeping the nation, it is certainly worthy of broad dissemination. Focusing on the inherent flaws of standardized testing to assess the value of affirmative action is, however, a grave mistake. We agree with the premise that our society falls far short of a true meritocracy, but find it hard to agree with the premise that our society functions as a true testocracy either. How many jobs really use standardized paper-and-pencil tests as the key method for hiring? A recent study of a nationally selective sample of U.S. firms found that only about 10 percent required an intelligence test to screen applicants for employment.[1] Probably the most common employment test is the simple typing test, one form of testing that is, arguably, both functional and fair. But even this form of assessment is never used alone, and is typically paired with educational credentials (evidence of past performance) and a face-to-face interview to assess appearance, demeanor, attitude, and so forth.

In educational admissions standardized testing clearly plays a greater role. But even in undergraduate, law, and medical school admissions, tests are only one of a number of factors taken into account. The authors' own example of University of Pennsylvania Law School admissions shows that only half of the law school class was chosen automatically based on LSAT and college grades. If tests really determined admission, we could fire all of our admissions committees tomorrow and have computers select incoming classes.

We think it is important to remember that standardized tests were instituted to increase fairness and open opportunities in the face of selection processes that operated via subjective assessments and closed networks bound by class, race, ethnicity, and gender. While tests are not perfectly fair, Sturm and Guinier vastly oversimplify their effects. Tests are a double-edged sword. The use of SATs made it possible for Jews educated in public schools to compete with moneyed applicants from prep schools for entry into elite universities.[2] Standardized tests enable women police officers to legally challenge the decisions of their superiors when they repeatedly pass over the higher-scoring females to promote male candidates.[3] A survey of private firms in Los Angeles, Detroit, Chicago, and Boston in the late 1980s and early 1990s shows that when tests were used as important screening devices in hiring decisions, African American employment rates were higher than when interviews were used.[4]

Sturm and Guinier are correct to point out that test scores today more often legitimate existing class and race inequality, and that small and essentially meaningless differences in test scores are used to differentiate among candidates who are functionally identical in skill, talent, and ability. The authors propose to replace these flawed tests with different strategies for leveling the playing field. Take, for instance, the idea that we determine admission to our best colleges by taking the top 1 percent of graduates from every high school in the country and then doing a weighted lottery. The lottery would be weighted to ensure representation from major racial and ethnic groups and to ensure equal numbers of men and women.

What would be the result? Many youngsters from poor schools with weaker educational backgrounds would win admission to our top colleges, and perhaps some would not succeed. But such a group would most definitely include individuals from diverse racial and socioeconomic backgrounds who have demonstrated the drive, determination, and ambition to succeed. To be the valedictorian of the high school in Wellesley or Weston takes a great deal of effort and intelligence, but to be the valedictorian in Chelsea or East Boston takes all of that plus an enormous determination to overcome considerable obstacles. Who will do better after four years in one of our best universities? The students who did what their parents, teachers, and neighbors supported and expected of them, or the students who succeeded despite overcrowded classrooms, indifferent adults, violent communities, chaotic learning environments, and the added pressure of after-school jobs or family responsibilities? As a selection method, this approach seems a superior way to tap into the drive, talent, and ambition of all our young citizens rather than those from already privileged homes.

UNDERSTANDING THE PERFORMANCE GAP

CLAUDE M. STEELE

I applaud Guinier and Sturm's efforts to shift the debate about selection away from a test-centered model. It is important, however, that people realize this shift is not an evasive one, motivated to avoid holding minority students to the same standards as everyone else. It is a shift that recognizes real limitations in a testing system, limitations, tied to race, that if not avoided can cause an unjustified discrimination against minority students.

Considerable research shows that standardized tests advantage applicants from better-off socioeconomic backgrounds, that they are not particularly strong predictors of subsequent performance, and that admissions committees should use them with caution, and then only together with as much information about candidates as can be obtained. But there are reasons to believe that this advice is especially important in the case of minorities. My own research, and that of my colleagues over the last twelve years, has shown that there are effects of race on test performance that go beyond any effects of socioeconomic disadvantage, affecting even the best-prepared, most-invested students from these groups who often come from middle-class backgrounds. While our research has focused on school admission and performance, I believe our findings can be applied to the workplace as well.

Through our research we have isolated a factor that can depress the standardized test performance of any group whose abilities are negatively stereotyped in the larger society: women taking difficult math tests; lower-class French students taking a difficult language exam; older people taking a difficult memory test; white male athletes being given a test of natural athletic ability; white males taking a difficult math test on which they are told "Asians do better"; as well as Hispanic students at the University of Texas being given a difficult English test.

We call this factor stereotype threat, and it refers to the experience of being in a situation where one recognizes that a negative stereotype about one's group is applicable to oneself. When this happens, one knows that one could be judged or treated in terms of that stereotype, or that one could inadvertently do something that would confirm it. We have found that in situations where one cares very much about one's performance or related outcomes—as in the case of serious students taking the SAT—this threat of being negatively stereotyped can be so upsetting and distracting that it directly interferes with performance.

In the case of minority students the effects of stereotype threat are striking. We often assume that once a situation is objectively the same for different groups, as in the case of "standardized" tests, it is *experienced* the same by each group. But for black students, unlike white students, the experience of difficulty on the test makes the negative stereotype about their group relevant as an interpretation of their performance, and of them. Thus they know as they meet frustration that they are especially likely to be seen through the lens of the stereotype as having limited ability. For those black students who care very much about performing well, this is a serious intimidation, implying, as it does, that they may not belong in the walks of life where the tested abilities are important, walks of life in which they are heavily invested. Like many pressures it may not be fully conscious, but it may be enough to impair their best thinking.

To test this idea, Joshua Aronson and I asked black and white Stanford students into our laboratory. We had statistically equated both groups on ability level and gave them a very difficult thirty-minute verbal test. Black students performed dramatically worse than did white students. We then selected another group of black and white students, again statistically equated on ability level, and presented them with the same test we had used before—this time not as a test of their "aptitude," but as a "problem-solving" task that had nothing to do with ability. A simple instruction, but it profoundly changed the meaning of the situation. It told black participants that the racial stereotype about their ability was irrelevant to their performance on this particular task. As a result, black students' performance on this test matched the performance of equally qualified whites. We found that the stereotype threat seemed to characterize the daily experiences of black students on predominantly white campuses and in predominantly white society, and directly affected important intellectual performances.

We have also discovered that the detrimental effect of stereotype threat on test performance is greatest for those students who are the most invested in doing well on the test. Across our research, stereotype threat most impaired students who were the most identified with achievement, those who were also the most skilled, motivated, and confident.

These findings make a point of some poignance: the characteristics that expose this vanguard to the pressure of stereotype threat are not weaker academic identity and skills, but stronger academic identity and skills. They have long seen themselves as good students, better than most other people. But led into the domain by their strengths, they pay an extra tax on their investment there, a "pioneer tax," if you will, of worry and vigilance that their futures will be compromised by the ways society perceives and treats their group. And it is paid every day, in every stereotype-relevant situation.

This has broader effects too. Stereotype threat follows its targets on to campus, affecting behaviors of theirs that are as varied as participating in class, seeking help from faculty, contact with students in other groups, and so on. And as it becomes a chronic feature of one's school environment, it can cause what we have called "disidentification"; the re-alignment of one's self-concept and values so that one's self-regard no longer depends on how well one does in that environment. Disidentification relieves the pain of stereotype threat by breaking identification with the part of life where the pain occurs, which necessarily includes a loss of motivation to succeed in that part of life.

So when we return to the charge that minority students are less "qualified" because of lower test scores, I hope that my research and that of others put the gaps in test performance in a different light: even ostensibly significant gaps in scores (300 points on the SAT, for example) can actually represent small differences in the real skills needed to get good college or law school grades. Moreover, they can reflect the influence of factors that are tied to race in our society but that are unrelated to real academic potential. Furthermore, these gaps are almost never caused by there being a lower admissions threshold for black than for whites or Asians. Test scores of blacks are taken as a sign of their being underprepared when, in fact, virtually all black students on a given campus have tested skills completely "above threshold" within the range of the tested skills for other students on the campus, and in this sense, have skills up to the competition.

All these findings, then, taken together, constitute a powerful reason for treating standardized tests as having limited utility as a measure of academic potential of students from these groups. Relying on these tests too extensively in the admissions process could preempt the admission of a significant portion of highly qualified minority students. It is simply the case that we have no single, or even small, set of indicators that satisfactorily captures "merit" or "potential" for academic success and a contributing life. And beyond reducing the significance of standardized tests as Guinier and Sturm suggest, our research makes clear that the subsequent challenge to a more fair selection process is the creation of safe and supportive environments in which talented and invested students can flourish.

Another problem is that gross categories like race and gender have a considerable heterogeneity within them. A great deal of evidence suggests that under current affirmative action programs recent immigrants and the children of immigrants are fulfilling many targets for racial diversity, leaving behind African-Americans and Puerto Ricans. Affirmative action has also noticeably failed in taking into account class origins. Both working-class African-Americans and working-class whites are woefully underrepresented in our elite schools and workplaces.

Devising alternate methods for giving members of these disadvantaged groups the opportunity to acquire and demonstrate skills would begin to broaden the reach of affirmative action into these difficult-to-reach segments of society. In addition to changing requirements for college admissions, Sturm and Guinier suggest an alternate selection strategy for employment decisions. They propose that above a certain floor of minimum qualifications for a job there should be a weighted lottery that assigns applicants to existing openings. These new hires would then have a probationary period in which they would be able to grow into the job, learn new skills, and demonstrate the aptitudes and abilities to meet the demands of the position. Sturm and Guinier argue that this new method would open positions to individuals who would previously not make the cut based on standardized testing.

But it is foolish to ignore the historical reason so many groups fought to implement standardized testing in the first place. When managers, college admissions officers, and bosses assess and evaluate the skills, talents, and abilities of individuals, there is a powerful opening for the operation of conscious or unconscious biases rooted in the racial, ethnic, class, and gender identities of both parties. The plain fact is that there is no silver bullet that removes socially embedded preferences from the decisions of human beings. The Sturm-Guinier proposal moves the crucial hiring decision to a post-hire evaluation based on job performance during the period of probation. But what is to keep a male manager from deciding that a female trainee did not grow into the job as effectively as the male trainee who, in his view, seems more suited to the job? Sturm and Guinier imply that somehow work evaluation is inherently more objective than decisions based on interviews. Although they acknowledge that who does the evaluation matters, and state that it is important to have diversity in those doing the evaluations, they do not explain how, absent affirmative action, this diversity will be achieved. If the premise of the new model is that these probationary hires will be evaluated by diverse teams of managers, it is hard to see how this would be ensured, if not through current legal and cultural values of affirmative action.

The promise of Sturm and Guinier's approach comes if it is seen not as a replacement for, but as an addition to, current affirmative action programs. Their proposal needs affirmative action in order to work because at its heart their proposal necessitates subjective assessments of work and education quality. Without diversity among managers, administrators, and teachers, the situation for women and minorities could actually be worse under the Sturm and Guinier proposal than it is now. Combining their proposal with the existing legal framework of affirmative action, however, might actually better deliver on the original promise of affirmative action programs—increasing both opportunities for individuals and true diversity in organizations.

TOO FORMAL?

PAUL OSTERMAN

Susan Sturm and Lani Guinier are driven by a concern for continued racial and gender-based inequities and are worried that affirmative action, as we know it, is proving an inadequate solution. Rather than use affirmative action to make amends around the edges, they want to rethink selection processes in general. Their characterization of the current state of play is that the "present system measures merit through scores on paper-and-pencil tests," and this is broadly unfair in both educational and employment settings. They believe that the approach they propose will not only lead to more equitable outcomes but will also help overcome the political opposition to affirmative action as practiced today.

I am very sympathetic to the objectives and underlying premises of this article. I agree that the distribution of rewards, economic and otherwise, in America is blatantly unfair and that an important element of this unfairness lies in racial and gender-based discrimination. I also agree that current selection and sorting processes should not be taken for granted. Having said this, I also think that the arguments made by Sturm and Guinier suffer from some problems of fact and logic that undermine their case.

* * *

My first worry is that their characterization of testing is wrong. It is weak both for its mischaracterization of the validity of tests and also for its exaggeration of the role tests play in admissions and in hiring. My second concern is that the solution they propose ignores some important lessons from research on organizational processes and is open to very substantial abuse against the groups they seek to protect.

Their argument that tests such as the SAT do a poor job of predicting performance is, I think, wrong. The Armed Forces Qualifying Test (AFQT), an SAT-like test that measures achievement (not ability or IQ) validly predicts job performance in the military, and a recent National Academy of Science report found that its reliability did not vary by race. With respect to the SAT itself, the research evidence shows that within a given institution (for example, Yale) the SAT has not predicted who does well. However, it seems problematic to argue that the SAT is not useful in predicting who will do well at Yale versus at a third-tier college. That is, if I ask you about two people, one of whom has an SAT score of 1500 and the other 1000, and you knew nothing else about these people, it would not be hard to guess who has the higher probability of getting better grades at Yale if they were both admitted.

But why should we be denied all other knowledge about the applicants? Isn't this exactly the authors' point, that more subtle acceptance processes should be used? But, of course, they already are. No selective college admits simply on the basis of SAT scores and almost all would consider other factors—such as family circumstances, the nature of the high school the students attended, and motivation—that might mitigate the poor SAT. This is part of the reason why within an institution the SAT has little predictive power. Nonetheless, at the end of the day and in conjunction with these other considerations the SAT will still help discriminate between candidates for Yale and for a third-tier college.

This is not, of course, to deny that the admissions criteria should be reconsidered. After all, in addition to family circumstances and motivation, colleges also consider such dubious criteria as legacy and the likelihood that the family will decide to finance a building. There is room for improvement, but the authors substantially overstate their case. Indeed, their very claim that we live in a "testocracy," at least when race is considered, is wrong. Selective colleges typically consider racial diversity and give less weight to the test results of underrepresented groups, as William Bowen and Derek Bok have made clear in their research on admissions.[1]

This overstatement is reinforced by the other canonical example Sturm and Guinier use, the civil service test. In this world, at least in the stereotyped view, the only hiring criterion is test scores, with hiring taking place from the top of the list, and affirmative action is thus vulnerable to being seen as unfair. However, it is difficult to think of any other jobs with a hiring procedure like this (and even the civil service doesn't really work in this manner—consider veterans' preferences). For virtually all jobs, particularly the "high-stakes" jobs the authors are concerned with, the hiring process already considers a mix of factors, just as colleges do in their admissions process. In the vast majority of today's labor market, formal tests play a much weaker role in hiring than the authors imply.

While much of the setup for the article is centered on tests and the problems surrounding them, the fact is that in most private sector jobs tests are not at the core of hiring or promotion. Instead, the procedures are much more informal—as is illustrated by the case of Bernice cited by Sturm and Guinier. They argue that through a combination of luck and openness to informal consideration of new criteria, Bernice was given a chance that she would not have had under the old system. But the old system, as the authors describe it, was also informal and judgment-based. It's just that a different set of criteria was part of the informality. So, in effect, the authors want to substitute one set of informal criteria and procedures for another.

The standards that Sturm and Guinier want to deploy are attractive and are in tune with an important current of modern ideas about assessment and multiple intelligences. If we use the idea of tests in a more generic sense, to refer to hiring criteria, then I agree with them that organizations should be more flexible about what they consider. In fact, many employers are already increasingly using nontraditional criteria. Research on hiring practices in so called high-performance work organizations shows that those firms that are implementing work teams and quality circles put heavy emphasis on interpersonal skills and initiative, and that they get at these via multiple interviews and role playing, including the involvement of current employees in selecting new ones.

But there are some further dangers, which should give us pause. First, research on organizations, such as the work of Barbara Reskin, suggests that outcomes are better for women and minorities when hiring and promotion procedures are formalized and not left to informal processes, which are vulnerable to abuse. Yet, in the authors' words, their proposals are "interactive and informal" and "rely explicitly on discretion and subjectivity." Not only does this run the risk highlighted by the research on organizational processes, but also seems to endanger the criteria of transparency and fairness that Sturm and Guinier lay out in their attack on traditional affirmative action and their sketch of the characteristics of a more desirable system. I think much more careful thought is needed to reconcile these concerns with the advantages of the approach they advocate and those being adopted by cutting-edge firms.

For all these reasons, Sturm and Guinier fail to make as compelling a case as they might wish for their conclusions. Nevertheless, I must say that I basically think that their bottom line is right. Outcomes are unfair. So are the processes that generate them. Diversity has very substantial payoffs both for individuals and organizations. We need to find ways to legitimize diversity as one consideration, among others, in school admissions and in job market decisions. What we also need to do, however, is to think through carefully how to get there. It is possible that the current practice of, in effect, giving some additional "points" to target groups in admissions or hiring is a reasonable way to proceed.

IT'S STILL A TEST

MAUREEN A. SCULLY AND DEBORAH M. KOLB

Sturm and Guinier present a persuasive case for why testing fails as a fair and credible gauge of merit. In their new approach to selection and inclusion in the workplace, they focus on actual performance on the job as "the best evidence of the ability to perform." They propose that a period of demonstrating competence and growing into a position should give women and minorities greater opportunities to display their merits and should avert the biases, scars, and resentments that surround tests. At the Center for Gender in Organizations, we study the workplace to see how the dynamics of difference play out for women and minorities, in ways that impact both equity and the effectiveness with which work gets done. We explore what the experience of the "extremely interactive and extended selection process" might be like and how it might still be a test, though a test of a different sort.

Consider the case of Bernice, the woman who, as Sturm and Guinier explain, became general counsel of a corporation after sharing the job with two other lawyers for nine months on a temporary basis. She networked with top executives who might not otherwise have seen her in action, showed her mettle by handling crises effectively, and discovered and honed her skills as a team player. To her surprise, she made the "final cut," and was offered the position.

This vignette has several features of interest. All eyes are on Bernice. This pressure might not bring out the best in some candidates (indeed, the fact that Bernice does not really perceive this period as an audition and is surprised at her "win" might be a significant reason for her successful performance). She has to prove herself in a difficult situation in which the criteria are unclear and emergent. The audition has some high stakes. In essence, "it's still a test."

And Bernice could trip up on this test in a number of ways. Knowing that she is being watched, she may be concerned about performance, not just her own, but of the group she manages. In our research, we have noticed how being "under the microscope" can cause people to micromanage and tightly control work. Bernice might engage in this behavior, unrepresentative of her true style, as a form of self-protection. But it could be read by others as evidence that she lacks the delegation skills critical for a leader. She will likely be conservative in her actions and avoid taking risks because she is being watched closely. Thus, she might be rated as failing to demonstrate the risk taking that is regarded as the mark of leadership.

It's also possible that Bernice will actually demonstrate the special kinds of skills that she can bring to the job, based on her different socialization and standpoint. For example, if she does not know that she is being observed for a promotion, she might practice her own style of coachlike and team-oriented leadership. But top executives, especially if they are a relatively homogenous group, might not see all the benefits this style brings to her work, and might be looking for traditional top-down leadership style instead. In addition, the rules of the game can shift along the way. If there is ambiguity about what constitutes high-level job performance, the pressures to conform spill over into the dress, speech, and demeanor that the contenders under scrutiny are expected to display. If Bernice does not play golf, are her job prospects subtly diminished during this extended test?

Finally, after attaining a position, a candidate from a different background might start to act more like herself, and perhaps make changes that enable the organization to appreciate different and needed types of merit or encourage other women and minorities. Or she might feel compelled to follow the norms of her predecessors. For a lone member of a minority group, the test is never really over. And if the two men who lost this contest to Bernice still bear the familiar resentment that she got the job because she was a woman, then the scrutiny and conformity pressures might feel even more intense. Under these circumstances, it will not be easy to change the organization from the top down.

Rethinking the use of tests is at the heart of this provocative and important essay. We agree, and suggest rethinking even the subtle, elongated, and high-pressure tests that might arise from the proposed alternative. All such tests are still anchored in a world of ranking, contests, and pyramid-shaped hierarchies, with fewer and fewer plum jobs as one approaches the top. Making the tests fairer and more closely linked to actual performance is a first-order fix.

A deeper fix is to rethink tests in all their various forms and the very shape and assumptions of structures that require such testing and selection games. For example, at Bernice's organization, the nine-month period when three people shared the general counsel job suggests a promising alternative. Job sharing and teams of equals diminish some of the pressures to pick one winner. They enable a mix of different work styles and types of merit to be developed and appreciated without the undercurrent of competition. Job sharing and teamwork can also promote other important ends, like giving employees more time to spend in their family and civic life. The prospects for such changes should not be oversimplified. But they suggest a method of looking at how work gets done, taking the counterproductive politics of competition into account, and using opportunistic moments—like the formation of the three-person general counsel office prompted by a merger—as triggers for small wins that could lead to bigger organizational changes.

DIVERSITY AND CAPITALISM

MICHAEL J. PIORE

I find this essay troublesome. I have almost no difficulty with the argument when taken one line at a time. But its basic thrust seems misguided. Sturm and Guinier lay out a new basis for an affirmative action public policy in employment and education by setting up "merit" as an independent policy objective. This seems to point toward a set of government policies that would likely be even more cumbersome and invasive than the policies already in place (although they never discuss specific policy). Moreover, recasting equal opportunity in their terms would obscure the original justification for affirmative action and make the existing policy almost incomprehensible to a generation of Americans who were born after the policies were in place and are increasingly the sons and daughters of immigrants whose families were not even in this country at that time.

Historically, equal employment opportunity policy arose as part of an attempt to dismantle a social system that systematically sought to stigmatize certain social groups and confine them to subordinate and demeaning social roles. It began as an effort to dismantle the system of white supremacy and discrimination against blacks, and was then extended to the system of male supremacy and discrimination against women. Ultimately, it has been used—or discussed—in relation to other ethnic and racial minorities, as well as the physically handicapped and gay men and lesbians. Whether or not white supremacy or male dominance remains a sufficient threat to justify the continuation of the policy, and whether or not the other systems of dominance and subordination are sufficiently invidious to warrant its extension, are debatable. But that, it seems to me, is the debate we need to have. All of these systems of dominance and subordination are of course nonmeritocratic, but in exactly the same sense that genocide is murder.

I also have trouble with the way Sturm and Guinier lay out the issue of meritocracy. It is not clear what they mean by merit. It appears to mean "economic performance," or relative economic performance. They are careful to distinguish between test scores and economic performance—indeed that is a major point of their article. But they seem to imply that test scores are the primary criteria for judging economic performance on the job, or for predicting it. I know of no precise figures on how employment is allocated, but test scores are certainly not the dominant allocative mechanism; in high-level jobs they are rarely used at all. The authors also distinguish between actual economic performance and the performance that would be possible if the job structure and technology were to be reoriented to take greater advantage of "diversity," but here too it is unclear operationally what this might mean. I believe, in fact, that the economy is being reorganized and reoriented in just this way—but not toward the kind of diversity that is central to the social problems with which Sturm and Guinier are concerned.

I do not see reward on the basis of relative economic performance as an independent moral principle. Much, if not most, of the difference in economic performance among individuals is due to traits that have nothing to do with the basic "worth" of people, such as intelligence, physical prowess, beauty, or social characteristics. Parents pass these traits on directly, or through the education that they enable their children to obtain.

Reward on the basis of relative economic performance is, however, arguably *instrumental* in the pursuit of principles that are moral. The argument that it is instrumental in this way is that it creates a more efficient economic system, one that maximizes national income and, hence, material well-being. That income, once it has been generated, can then be redistributed in accordance with whatever set of principles do have moral validity.

The optimal institutional structure for achieving such a system is a competitive market economy. In such an economy, the agents have a strong incentive to allocate jobs on the basis of relative economic performance because they are rewarded for doing so by higher returns and, in the extreme, punished for failing to do so by bankruptcy. Those agents, moreover, operate at a level where they have the maximum information required to distinguish among individual workers. If they nonetheless fail to allocate jobs on the basis of merit, it may be because the differences in merit among people are small relative to the costs of making those distinctions among them, or because the distinctions simply cannot be made at all. In any case, if employers cannot make this distinction when they are close to the job and under strong market pressure to do so, I doubt very much that an external agent would be able to do so. The kind of surveillance involved in trying to do so, is, moreover, very costly and invasive, as we have learned in the pursuit of race and sex discrimination. Exactly what the relationship is (or was) between these social systems of domination and subordination and the competitive marketplace has never been precisely clear. What is clear is that the systems, and the mechanisms and belief structures through which they were promulgated and maintained, completely overwhelmed whatever competitive pressure might have countervailed them. There is no reason to believe that they would have disappeared without the kinds of equal employment policies we have pursued in the last three decades. It is not clear that these polices, however costly and invasive, have been sufficient to eliminate the problem. But the compromises the market made on race and sex—compromises that virtually every institution in our society also made—do not invalidate presumptions in favor of the market in general.

Finally, I think there are special dangers in linking the case for equal employment opportunity to the efficiency of diversity. The success of the American economy in the 1990s *is* arguably due to the increasing diversity of its workforce. Certainly, company by company, the labor force in the high-tech industries, which have fueled the expansion and restored the country to a preeminent position in global markets, is probably the most ethnically diverse in the world. The diversity has probably contributed to the success of these companies in several ways: it has made it possible for them to draw upon a high-quality, extremely flexible labor force; it has contributed to the creative tensions that foster the development of new and innovative products; and it has made the companies more attuned to the foreign markets in which these products are sold. Many of these factors can be measured, and eventually it will become possible to test the contribution of diversity to economic performance of companies in a relatively precise way. There is already a movement in this direction within the accounting profession as part of the effort to better reflect the role of high-level human resources in the value of particular companies in the new economy.

The diversity of these high-tech companies is the direct product of the openness of our system of higher education to foreign students and faculty and to the changes in our immigration laws in the 1960s. The openness of education and immigration were undoubtedly facilitated by the ideology of tolerance and diversity, which grew out of the country's response to the civil rights movement. *But* the diversity in these companies is concentrated among certain groups (such as Asian Americans and recent immigrants) at the expense of other racial minorities (such as native-born blacks), and probably of native-born women as well. The latter groups are not well represented in the diverse labor force of the high-tech industries, and without the new immigration there would be a great deal more economic pressure to facilitate their upward mobility. Thus, while the ideology of diversity may ultimately contribute to economic success, and that ideology is bound up with the forces that have promoted equal employment opportunity, the diversity that has contributed to success at the level of the firm does not have much to do with the groups that have been the target of equal opportunity policies.

PSEUDO-MERITOCRACY

PETER SACKS

Americans harbor the collective deceit that most of the necessary academic attributes of schools, schoolchildren, applicants to colleges and universities, and even prospective employees can be neatly summed up with a single number—a test score. Defenders of this system call it meritocracy. More likely it's a pseudo-meritocracy, governed by a cult of measurement and the triumph of technocratic thinking.

Many Americans believe in the comforting illusion that test scores permit their important institutions to rank, rate, and sort schools, students, and job applicants with nearly infallible precision. The numbers don't lie—or so we like to think.

What's more, we've created a postmodern oddity in which one's *potential* for real-life achievement in school or work has become more powerful and real than one's actual achievement. We tend to forget that standardized tests are but distant and abstruse abstractions of the real world and all its rich complexity.

Consider the case of Carmello Melendez, who came to the United States from Puerto Rico as a child and who encountered a lifetime of stigmatization and exclusion because of his poor test scores, both on achievement tests for school and aptitude tests for the military. He nevertheless excelled at every job he got a chance to perform—from host and producer of public affairs television to civil rights investigator.

Melendez applied for a job as urban affairs manager with Illinois Bell. He was exceedingly well qualified for the job but missed the cutoff score on Illinois Bell's aptitude test for managers. Ninety percent of whites, but just 57 percent of Hispanics and African Americans, passed this test. Ample evidence showed the test was essentially worthless for predicting job performance—about as good as throwing dice—and yet the company continued to rely on the test as a gatekeeper for employment. Like so many other institutions, Illinois Bell believed that job applicants should be ranked based on the smallest differences in test scores, and that such a ranking was absolutely indicative of one's professional competence—despite real and proven track records in school and the workplace.

Meanwhile, many institutions have been compelled to "fix" their gatekeeping systems with a Band-Aid that we've come to call affirmative action. When a democratic society can't tolerate a "whiteout" of its important academic and corporate institutions, because of gatekeeping rules that block access to many minorities, then those rules must be modified.

But instead of changing the system for all citizens, and rethinking the very meaning of *merit* in this society, colleges and universities have chosen to adopt two sets of gate-keeping rules, one for whites and Asians, and one for blacks and Hispanics. Indeed, the existence of two-tiered gate-keeping systems has been the focal point of the recent legal attacks on affirmative action, from California's Proposition 209 to the *Hopwood* case in Texas.

That colleges and universities themselves continue to defend affirmative action as the chief means to diversify their campuses is laudable, and not a little curious. While affirmative action policies do, in essence, diminish the importance of test scores for some college aspirants, the prevailing and entrenched hegemony of test scores—the final "objective" arbiter of who has merit and who doesn't—continues to thrive for the vast majority of admissions decisions.

Surely, implementing affirmative action has been a necessary and good fight, which has helped to redress higher education's past sins of exclusion. But I am in wholehearted agreement with Sturm and Guinier: defenders of race-based preferences—and Americans generally—have *judiciously sidestepped the larger question of the legitimacy of the nation's prevailing notions of merit.* Why have we failed to fully engage that question?

A persuasive circumstantial case can be made that affirmative action is a useful tool of American elites, which enables them to preserve a social definition of merit that primarily serves their own economic interests. Even with affirmative action, the vast majority of the admissions remain subject to the prevailing views about merit that primarily benefit children of the well educated and well-to-do, even at public institutions.

The law school at the University of California at Los Angeles is a remarkable case in point. Even with the help of its affirmative action program in the early 1990s, it relied on the usual numerical index of test scores and grades for most students—resulting in a student body with a socioeconomic profile that mirrored the upper crust of American society. The students' fathers had graduate degrees considerably more often than the average American father; their mothers were far more likely to have obtained bachelor's degrees. Their parents' income was more than double the national median.

Institutions often look the other way, but the research evidence is overwhelming that gatekeeping tests are not objective, fair, or accurate, and that they amount to artificial and arbitrary barriers for some Americans and keys to the kingdom for others.

Some defenders of affirmative action counter that ending affirmative action as we know it would, in effect, spell doom for academic standards at America's colleges and universities. Race-blind admissions, this specious reasoning suggests, would by necessity mean reduced admissions standards applied to everyone, thus lowering average SATs, GREs, and LSATs, and diminishing the intellectual stature of the nation's coveted system of higher education.

But there's ample reason to suspect that a world without

affirmative action, if it also shunned the prevailing ideology of merit, would not be apocalyptic. With what we know about the present system's failure to judge human potential—the lion's share of the variation in people's achievement is *not* accounted for by test scores and grades—we can take comfort in knowing that changing the gatekeeping rules for all college-bound Americans will not measurably erode academic quality.

Indeed, there may be a silver lining with regard to ending affirmative action as we know it. For, as colleges and universities struggle to reinvent themselves, and to institutionalize far broader and more complete perspectives of merit, educational quality may be poised for a new renaissance in America. This renewal of the meritocracy may come not at the cost of racial and ethnic diversity, but may actually enhance the goals of affirmative action and equal opportunity.

WHAT'S FAIR?

PETER CAPPELLI

Arguments about affirmative action have often been based on misinformation about how applicants are selected in the "real" world. Susan Sturm and Lani Guinier are doing important work in developing an argument for affirmative action that is based on more accurate information about how selection works. Their argument focuses on the selection decisions used in hiring, in admissions to education, and in promotions, and it begins by challenging the implicit assumption that those who are selecting applicants know what they are doing.

It is certainly reasonable to argue that organizations have a right to select the best and most capable applicants. But in many cases, they make no rigorous attempt to do so. Most organizations (including university faculties) make hiring decisions based on unstructured interviews, despite the documented fact that interviews are about the worst method for determining which candidates will make good employees. Perceptions of applicant ability based on the typical method of unstructured interviews have roughly zero correlation with subsequent performance in jobs. Many employers appear to have no systematic arrangements for selecting among applicants.

What may be more surprising is that even systematic attempts to determine who will be a good employee or a successful student are far from accurate. Selection tests and college admission tests are limited to predicting performance in first jobs and first-semester grade point averages, respectively. Even the very best of these tests correlate at levels less than 50 percent with actual performance and most predict far less (even 50 percent correlational relationships translate into predicting only 25 percent of the variance in performance). If employers or higher education institutions cannot tell which applicants are going to be good, then the common objection to affirmative action—that giving preference in admissions or hiring to members of a protected group will in some way hurt the organization by excluding better applicants—is substantially weakened.

The strongest argument against this common objection to affirmative action comes from empirical results about what affirmative action actually does in practice. A recent and important survey of this literature by Harry Holzer and David Neumark reaches several noteworthy conclusions.[1] First, affirmative action seems to work in the sense that it promotes distributive justice—that is, it increases employment or participation among women and minorities in the organizations that use it. Second, employers who engage in affirmative action seem to recruit and select more carefully—that is, they look more broadly for applicants and evaluate them against more criteria. Finally, and most important, these employers do not appear to pay any price in terms of employee performance for engaging in affirmative action. In fact, the job performance of women and minorities hired by these employers is, if anything, higher than that of white males. Despite the fact that the credentials on characteristics like education are lower for the women and minority employees of firms that pursue affirmative action, their employers seem to have uncovered other attributes about them, through more careful recruiting, that are associated with better job performance.

The argument that affirmative action is at a minimum no worse than the alternative from the perspective of employers seems on solid ground. If the methods that employers are using now have an adverse impact on protected groups, as Sturm and Guinier assert, and employers are not getting much from those methods, then the argument for affirmative action, which has the considerable advantage of enhancing distributive justice, is very powerful.

But what if the alternative here is not typical recruitment and selection practices? What if employers got more sophisticated and adopted the best selection procedures? Many of the best selection tests in terms of predictive power, such as cognitive ability tests, also seem to be ones that have the most adverse impact. Sturm and Guinier have a point in arguing that many paper-and-pencil tests seem to discriminate against minorities in particular. A recent study of higher education admissions and test scores confirms this point in showing that blacks score disproportionately lower on SAT tests than on other indicators of college performance, such as high school grades.[2] The same may be true for employment selection tests. Here they offer a sensible alternative: if other practices, perhaps in combination, can achieve the same level of predictive power while avoiding adverse impact, then those other practices should be preferred.

Their other recommendations may be harder to swallow, at least for most employers, because they do not seem to be based on how most employers operate. For example, it is no doubt true that some individuals may be able to perform jobs well in ways other than recruiters and employment test designers envision. But it is also difficult to ask organizations to let people who do not appear to be qualified try out jobs to see if they can succeed at them in different ways. The costs of failure for most jobs are big, not only the turnover costs if someone does not work out but also the potential costs of accidents and mistakes. The law also makes employers liable for hiring unqualified employees, for example, who cause accidents, if the employers did not take reasonable steps to screen them. Arrangements where otherwise unqualified applicants are hired and then trained and developed to handle jobs are a great idea for expanding opportunity, but are also a significant operating expense that not all employers are equipped to bear, especially in a just-in-time economy. Nor is there any reason to think that team-based, self-managed work systems will result in less discrimination. If employers discriminate, despite economic incentives to hire the best people and human resource departments trained to do otherwise, then there is no reason to think that individual employees will behave better. And while it is true that there are some advantages to a diverse workforce from the perspective of performance, there are also costs, and it is not obvious that the net effect is such that it will necessarily encourage decision makers to act in the interests of diversity.

It is worth bearing in mind that predicting who is going to be a good employee or a successful student or a good citizen is an enormously complicated exercise. It is difficult to do even after the fact, as anyone who has ever struggled with writing a performance appraisal can attest. There are other issues associated with hiring employees and admitting college students in addition to predicting who will succeed, of course, and these concern the issue of who gets ahead in society. As Sturm and Guinier make clear, it is much easier to argue for affirmative action to advance distributive justice if it does not conflict with the right of employers or other institutions to select individuals that serve the institutions purpose. And more valid arrangements that also advance affirmative action would be highly desirable.

It does still leave us, however, with a vexing problem of procedural justice, the right of applicants to be treated fairly. The standardized tests and civil service exams that Sturm and Guinier rightly criticize on validity grounds at least have the advantage of being objective and consistent for the applicants, if not necessarily valid from the perspective of the institutions administering them. Applications for sought-after and politically sensitive positions like civil service jobs or state university admissions are based on objective tests precisely to quell the procedural justice complaints—and lawsuits—that such decisions otherwise raise. A more diverse set of selection criteria that allow applicants to demonstrate competencies in different ways has the disadvantage of making the process appear less objective. One might well prefer a system that advances diversity while producing competent individuals to one that does neither but seems fair to the applicants, but it would obviously be best to achieve all three goals.

3

REPLY

SUSAN STURM AND LANI GUINIER

The issue of affirmative action continues to dominate the racial justice landscape. It frequently dictates the conceptual and policy framework for increasing access to education and employment. Its preservation has largely defined the strategy and goals of many civil rights organizations. Its operation often substitutes for a more comprehensive effort to address the fundamental structural distortions in the way we allocate educational and employment opportunities for everyone.

"The Future of Affirmative Action" is an effort to shift this preoccupation with affirmative action as the organizing framework for addressing access to education and employment, both generally and for women and people of color. Affirmative action is, in our view, a program, rather than a vision. It may be an appropriate short-term program, but it is not an adequately conceptualized long-term strategy for pursuing equity and efficacy in education and employment. Especially when affirmative action is the primary strategy for racial justice, it offers a narrow, at-the-margins response to exclusion, which deflects attention from more central problems with the current system for allocating access. Our goal is not, as Stephen Steinberg presumes, to replace "affirmative action as we know it," or to provide a substitute because courts have begun to invalidate traditional affirmative action programs. It is, instead, to shift the overall framework of the debate. We aim to develop a long-term, normative vision of racial justice that corresponds to present circumstance, that focuses attention on the underlying unfairness of current approaches to allocating access more generally, and that generates experiments in institutional redesign that can address problems at this more structural level.

The responses to our essay reveal the challenges we have yet to meet in this effort. One of the more intractable challenges, although the easiest conceptually, is to dislodge the prevailing commitment to short-term definitions of efficiency and merit. For example, quibbling with the validity of tests for predicting first-year performance in school largely misses the point. The central problem with tests' role in selection is how they are used—to rank-order applicants at the margins, to exclude applicants who could do as well, and to stand in for defining values and institutional goals. Our concern is who gets excluded despite each person's capacity to succeed, rather than whether those who perform well on tests are also screened for other traits. We believe that our institutions define value in ways that, as Howard Gardner puts it, are heavily skewed toward a few measurable "end states," often at the expense of more important values.

As Peter Sacks says, "the cult of measurement" and the "prevailing and entrenched hegemony of test scores" triumph over "one's actual achievement" in the real world. Like Sacks, Cappelli, Gardner, Bell, and Steele, we are not confident that those who do less well on high-stakes tests in fact do worse in school or on the job. Indeed, many tests exclude applicants who could in fact perform successfully. For example, a calibration error in scoring the Army Services Vocational Aptitude Battery resulted in the admission to the military of over 300,000 recruits who actually failed the screening test used by the armed services. In studies of the subsequent performance of those "ineligibles," predicted performance differentials did not materialize.[1]

Similarly, the Texas Ten Percent Plan, which admits the top 10 percent of the graduating class from every high school in the state, suggests that SAT-type tests exclude candidates who would be able to succeed. Peter Cappelli acknowledges this general claim—that high school grades have a less discriminatory impact—and suggests that alternative admission practices are a sensible option. His confidence is not misplaced, based on data from the first two years of the Texas program. Indeed, those admitted pursuant to the 10 percent standard, based on high school grades alone, actually outperform peers who were admitted based on traditional SAT-type tests. The 10 percenters have a higher freshman grade point average than those admitted using conventional criteria, apparently because the 10 percenters see themselves as successful, have drive and self-confidence, and are willing to seek help and ask questions when needed.

Claude Steele helps us understand the dynamics causing "real limitations in a testing system." Steele's pathbreaking work on stereotype threat shows that stereotypes, expectations, and racial dynamics can profoundly affect both the test-taking experience and the results. This work underscores the importance of test context, including the signals accompanying the test's administration and the institutional culture causing good students to withdraw or "disidentify" with the institution from which they originally sought an education. And it shifts our attention to creating institutional environments that encourage all students' full participation and high expectations.

We face a second challenge, which is to move the public conversation and practice beyond the traditional dichotomies, such as formal/informal, public/private, normative/ instrumental, racial justice/merit, that tend narrowly to construct our understanding of the universe of choices available for pursuing racial justice. For example, Stephen Steinberg and Paul Osterman argue that moving beyond dominant reliance on tests necessarily leads back to the systems of informal, subjective, and biased decision making that tests were in part developed to prevent. This concern is well founded, but in our view, unduly static and reactive. The approach to selection need not simply reflect a choice between these polar alternatives. We are urging interactive experimentation within institutions to permit more accountable and transparent decision making. It is our hope that—over time—such experiments will reveal best practices that make the inevitable exercise of discretion fair and functional. We have seen evidence that this can happen when companies and colleges replace fixed and rigid rules with dynamic and accountable processes that include more of the stakeholders.

Such institutionally based responses are increasingly crucial. The dynamics of "second-generation" racial and gender exclusion—bias resulting from patterns and structures of interaction—are often more complex, culturally embedded, and subtle. They do not necessarily emerge from the conduct that produced the first generation of inequality and activism. We appreciate Michael Piore's concern that unless we organize our remedial strategies around the original normative account of racial inequality, which was based on systematically and deliberately subordinating people of color and women, we necessarily abandon any principle of racial justice. But this account would place the more structural, second-generation forms of bias beyond the scope of either normative or legal inquiry. Complex conditions in today's workforce produce continuing racial and gender inequities and require structural solutions that are equally complex in their application and justification. The assumption that we must choose a single explanatory account to justify remedial intervention based on the conditions that prevailed when the civil rights laws were enacted, in our view, unnecessarily polarizes and constrains the choices facing those concerned with racial justice.

For this reason, we do not take the position that we should "end affirmative action as we know it." Indeed, because our goal was to shift public discourse, we did not explicitly take a position in the current affirmative action debate. We agree with the comments of Mary Waters, Deborah Kolb, and Maureen Scully, who suggest that racial and gender inclusion is a both/and proposition. Institutions that cannot, or will not, address the problem of racial and gender inclusion more structurally may need some form of affirmative action at least as a stopgap. The absence of diversity may be a valid critique justifying additional outreach and recruitment, including legal sanctions. But the presence of diversity—especially in its most superficial forms—is not alone a sufficient solution. Narrowly defined affirmative action programs are inadequate long-term solutions to problems of access, participation, and functionality. Sustainable solutions will require approaches that link issues of racial and gender justice to strategies for changing institutions, experimenting with new pedagogy, redefining long-term goals, and clarifying notions of democratic participation.

Derrick Bell reminds us of a third barrier to constructing a long-term vision of racial justice. Awareness of race—even when presented in the context of institutional fairness more generally—often triggers stereotypes and prompts myths that "supplant accuracy, logic and even common sense." Many working-class whites might also benefit from our systemic and institutional analysis, yet Bell warns that some who read our proposals will ignore the more general critique and reject our approach as "just a jazzed-up version of affirmative action." This polarizing effect apparently disables these respondents from hearing our structural critique and instead triggers in their minds a more conventional and formalistic antidiscrimination rhetoric. It is true that a few responses to our essay do appear to miss our fundamental point, but we continue to believe that the experience of those at the margins can help us to comprehend deficits in the structure as a whole. As a result, we are less despairing than Bell about the chances—over time—of changing the way people conceptualize problems of educational or job access.

The comments of Steele, Waters, Kolb, Scully, and Howard Gardner highlight a fourth important challenge for subsequent work: identifying and encouraging the development of workable ideas about how to allocate educational and employment opportunities. Mary Waters proposes a weighted lottery for the top 1 percent of high school students. Kolb and Scully demonstrate the promise of experimentation by transforming our performance-based test of Bernice into a new form of collaboration and teamwork in the workplace. Howard Gardner proposes using apprenticeships and technology to create opportunities to learn, and then to base future opportunities on how students make use of those opportunities. Claude Steele emphasizes the importance of creating environments that support full class participation, faculty mentoring, and involvement in valued activities. To be workable, any of these strategies may need to be implemented on an experimental basis to gain insight into their actual effect, not just their predicted effect, and to fine-tune them over time.

In addition, such strategies raise critical questions about how we choose to allocate scarce resources. Such questions can only be resolved by a much overdue debate on the mission of educational institutions in a multiracial democracy. Is the goal of our institutions of higher education simply to reward those who have already been given access to rich resources or is the goal of such institutions also to serve the democratic function of providing opportunity to those who can take advantage of it, who have been denied such opportunities in the past, and who are likely to use that opportunity to realize larger societal goals?

Some of these questions are more easily addressed in the workplace setting, where the mission of the institution is not contested. Indeed, Susan Sturm's current work has focused on workplace issues, where she documents and extrapolates from emerging experiments with structural approaches to racial and gender inclusion.[2] This work shows that forward-looking companies, non-governmental organizations, advocates, and courts have begun to develop more structural approaches that connect issues of racial and gender justice with broader institutional transformation. These examples establish that effective, legitimate, and accountable processes can emerge, and offer a way to develop contingent criteria that could assist in the evaluation of future processes.

For example, Deloitte & Touche, America's third-largest accounting, tax, and management-consulting firm, implemented a major Women's Initiative Program, which dramatically increased women's advancement in the company and reduced the turnover rate for women in particular and employees in general. The firm accomplished this by forming ongoing, participatory task forces, and giving them the responsibility to determine the nature and cause of the problem, make recommendations about how to address them, develop systems to address those problems, and then to monitor the results. The task force recommendations were implemented through ongoing data gathering and analysis, operational change through line management, and accountability in relation to benchmarks. This approach offers a structured set of opportunities for collective action by women's groups oriented around addressing problems of immediate and direct concern. The Women's Initiative produced swift and observable results, both in women's participation and in the firm's overall retention rate. The combination of increased communication and programmatic change contributed to what many called a culture change. Flexible work has become acceptable at Deloitte, for women and men.

Home Depot also faced the problem of how to minimize the expression of bias in a highly discretionary process of hiring and promotion, in a company that was dynamic, decentralized, and entrepreneurial. The solution was to achieve accountability through technology, information systems, and systematizing discretion, rather than through rules. The keystone of the new system is an automated hiring and promotion system, called the Job Preference Program. This process virtually eliminates the possibility for managers to steer applicants to particular roles based on stereotypes, expands the pool of applicants for every position, and opens up avenues for advancement that applicants themselves may not otherwise have considered.[3] As a result, rates of participation by women have risen and employee turnover rates have dropped across the company, not just in the divisions covered by the Consent Decree. People of color are participating at higher rates, even though they are not covered by the terms of the Consent Decree. And, the company has begun to track and use information from its Open Door Dispute Resolution system as a problem-solving tool.

Both examples illustrate the promise of, and need to learn from, experiments that use institutional innovation to pursue racial and gender equity, as a catalyst for more comprehensive institutional change. We mention them not as solutions, but as examples of the possibility of change—in how race and gender issues can be addressed to permit the structured and accountable exercise of discretion; in how institutions can actively define long-term goals and institute systems that enable those goals to be pursued and continually reevaluated; and in how racial and gender inclusion is connected to questions of institutional efficacy on one hand, and basic values of democratic participation on the other. It is not a coincidence that these examples come from the workplace rather than the educational arena. At least in some contexts, employers like Home Depot and Deloitte & Touche have been able to create a process for identifying their important goals and for relating the question of "who's qualified" to their broader institutional objectives. This makes it possible to construct ways of holding decision makers accountable, and to track bias in the allocation of opportunity. Home Depot embraced the concept of providing expert service and knowledge for purchasers of home improvement products. It then designed a method of matching and then tracking, applicants' qualifications and managers' decisions. The company created a computerized system of accountability that reveals managers who overlook women and people of color, and applicants who do not advance. This information prompts remedial plans, and is also used as part of the yearly evaluation of managers.

By contrast, many educational institutions have not been pushed to clarify their role in a multiracial democracy, and the determination of "who's qualified" is often isolated from the realization of long-term educational goals. Our final challenge stems from this inability of some educational institutions to struggle with the issue of institutional mission in conjunction with the development of innovative, inclusive, and more effective approaches to admissions, curriculum reform, and pedagogy.

This book is just a first step in encouraging many others to come forward to elaborate more fully the concrete possibilities and to ground conversations about affirmative action in commitments to institutional transformation and racial and gender justice. By broadening the conversation and reframing the debate, it is our hope that a larger constituency for change may materialize to reclaim affirmative action's innovative ideal.

NOTES

Susan Sturm and Lani Guinier / *The Future of Affirmative Action*

1. See *Johnson v. Transportation Agency*, 480 US 616 (1987); and *Wygant v. Jackson Board of Education*, 476 US 267 (1986). The most politicized version of the anti–affirmative action narrative is typified by the campaign strategy used by Sen. Jesse Helms, the white incumbent, against Harvey Gantt, his black challenger, in 1990. The Helms campaign commercial displayed a white working-class man tearing up a rejection letter while the voice-over said, "You needed that job, and you were the best qualified. . . . But it had to go to a minority because of a racial quota." See Andrew Hacker, *Two Nations: Black and White, Separate, Hostile, Unequal* (New York: Scribner, 1992), 202.

2. Laura K. Bass, "Affirmative Action: Reframing the Discourse" (unpublished manuscript, December 4, 1995).

3. No tester claims that the LSAT or the SAT, which is designed to predict academic performance, has ever been validated to predict job performance or pay. One study by Christopher Jencks finds that people who had higher-paying jobs also had higher test scores. One problem with this conclusion is that higher test scores were used to screen out applicants from earlier, formative opportunities. Another study, by David Chambers et al., of graduates of the University of Michigan Law School finds no correlation between the LSAT and either job satisfaction or pay.

4. See David K. Shipler, "My Equal Opportunity, Your Free Lunch," *New York Times*, 5 March 1995.

5. As Walter Willingham, an industrial psychologist who consults with the Educational Testing Service (the organization that prepares and administers the SAT), points out, leadership in an extracurricular

activity for two or more years is also a good proxy for academic performance, future leadership, and professional satisfaction.

6. "In all decades, those with higher index scores tend to make fewer social contributions . . . than those with lower index scores." See Richard O. Lempert, David L. Chambers, and Terry K. Adams, "The River Runs Through Law School," *Journal of Law and Social Inquiry* 25 (2000): 468. See also, William G. Bowen and Derek Bok, *The Shape of the River: Long-Term Consequences of Considering Race in College and University Admissions* (Princeton: Princeton University Press, 1998).

7. See Mary Anne C. Case, "Disaggregating Gender from Sex and Sexual Orientation: The Effeminate Man in the Law and Feminist Jurisprudence," *Yale Law Journal* 105 (1995): 88–89.

8. See the *Report of the Independent Commission on the Los Angeles Police Department*, 83–84. "Female LAPD officers are involved in excessive use of force at rates substantially below those of male officers. . . . The statistics indicate that female officers are not reluctant to use force, but they are not nearly as likely to be involved in use of excessive force," due to female officers' perceived ability to be "more communicative, more skillful at de-escalating potentially violent situations and less confrontational."

9. J. Phillip Thompson, director of management and operations for the New York City Housing Authority from 1992–93, told us that an internal evaluation conducted by the Housing Authority revealed that women housing authority officers were policing in a different, but successful, way. As a result of this evaluation, the authority sought to recruit new cops based on their ability to relate to young people, their knowledge of the community, their willingness to live in the housing projects, and their interest in police work. They also offered free housing to any successful recruit willing to live in the projects.

10. See James Crouse and Dale Trusheim, *The Case Against the SAT* (Chicago: University of Chicago Press, 1988), 128.

11. See Phyllis Rosser, *The SAT Gender Gap: Identifying the Causes* (Washington, D.C.: Center for Women's Policy Studies, 1989), 4. Also, "ETS Developing 'New' GRE," *FairTest Examiner,* Fall/Winter 1995–96, p. 11. "Research . . . shows the GRE under-predicts the success of minority students. And an ETS Study concluded the GRE particularly

under-predicts for women over 25, who represent more than half of female test-takers."

12. Crouse and Trusheim, *Case Against the SAT,* 103.

13. Ibid., 107–8.

14. See John G. Belcher, "Gainsharing and Variable Pay: The State of the Art," *Compensation & Benefits Review* 26 (May–June 1994): 50–51. Belcher advocates the use of a family of measures approach, which "utilizes multiple, independent measures to quantify performance improvement."

15. See, for example, Claude M. Steele and Joshua Aronson, "Stereotype Threat and the Intellectual Test Performance of African Americans," *Journal of Personality and Social Psychology* 69 (1995): 797–811.

16. Although there is debate about the degree of fundamental change in approaches to management, a significant portion of private businesses have adopted some form of collaborative or team-oriented production. See Edward E. Lawler III et al., *Employee Involvement and Total Quality Management: Practices and Results in Fortune 1000 Companies* (San Francisco: Jossey-Bass, 1992), which analyzes the employee-involvement programs many corporations have adopted; and Paul Osterman, "How Common Is Workplace Transformation and Who Adopts It?" *Industrial & Labor Relations Review* 47 (1994): 173, 176–78, which finds that over 50 percent of firms surveyed had introduced at least one innovation such as quality circles and work teams, and that 36.6 percent have at least two practices in place with at least 50 percent of employees involved in each.

17. Howard Gardner, *Multiple Intelligences: The Theory in Practice* (New York: Basic Books, 1993), 172.

18. See Karen W. Arenson, "Study Details Success Stories in Open Admissions at CUNY," *New York Times,* 7 May 1996. A study of open-admissions policy at City University of New York (CUNY) found that more than half of the students eventually graduated, even though it took many as long as ten years to do so. Many of these students had to work full-time while they attended college. According to Professor David Lavin, one of the co-authors of the CUNY study, open admissions "provided opportunities that students used well, and that translated into direct benefits in the job market and clearly augmented the economic base." Similarly, at Haverford College, professors of biology, chemistry,

and mathematics told one of us in interviews that many students of color with weak preparation in the natural sciences took two years to catch up with their better prepared peers. Then, by junior year, those same students managed to excel, having overcome their initial disadvantages.

19. When one of us was on the admissions committee in the early 1990s at the University of Pennsylvania Law School, the process of admitting people who had some "special" quality to be considered—which included being a poor, white chicken farmer from Alabama—was an openly deliberative process. It included students who knew more about the specific localities in which many of the applicants resided. The applications were redacted to eliminate personal identifying information but were otherwise available to the entire committee. The recommendations were read and considered (by contrast to the 50 percent of the class who were admitted solely on a mathematical equation based on their LSAT scores, their college rank, and the "quality" of their college as determined by the median LSAT score of its graduating class). In this process, the committee of faculty, students, and admissions personnel had a sense we were admitting a "class" of students, not just random individuals. Thus, we might give weight to some factors over others, depending upon the "needs" of the institution to have racial and demographic diversity, but also upon our commitment to fulfilling the needs of the profession to serve the entire public and to train private and public problem solvers who would become the next generation of leaders. Thus, not all students were admitted primarily because of their academic talents. We considered those who might be better oral advocates and eventual litigators. Others were already accomplished negotiators or future practitioners of alternative dispute-resolution practices. Students were not admitted if we felt they were unqualified to do the work demanded of them at the institution.

20. Gardner, *Multiple Intelligences*, 171–73.

21. She learned that she was proficient in skills that she did not previously identify as related to lawyering: problem solving, thinking about the public-relations management of crises, strategic planning, and dealing with internal disruption stemming from crisis and change.

22. For example, the court in *Hopwood v. Texas* rejected the concept of diversity as a basis for using affirmative action. The opinion lacked al-

most any reflection on the functional role diversity plays in higher education. It simply asserted that "the use of race, in and of itself, to choose students simply achieves a student body that looks different." 78 F.3d 932, 945 (Fifth Circuit, 1996), cert. denied, 116 S. Ct. 2582 (1996).

23. Jonathan D. Casper, "Restructuring the Traditional Civil Jury: The Effects of Changes in Composition and Procedures," in *Verdict: Assessing the Civil Jury System,* ed. Robert E. Litan (Washington, D.C.: Brookings Institution Press, 1993), 420.

24. See Susan P. Sturm, "From Gladiators to Problem Solvers: Women, the Academy, and the Legal Profession," *Duke Journal of Gender Law & Policy* (1996).

25. See Samuel L. Gaertner et al., "The Contact Hypothesis: The Role of a Common Ingroup Identity on Reducing Intergroup Bias," *Small Group Research* 25 (1994): 224, 226; and Samuel L. Gaertner et al., "How Does Cooperation Reduce Intergroup Bias?" *Journal of Personality & Social Psychology* 59 (1990): 692.

26. See Elizabeth Bartholet, "Application of Title VII to Jobs in High Places," *Harvard Law Review* 95 (1982): 947, 967–78, which discusses courts' reluctance to scrutinize high-level employment decisions; and Deborah L. Rhode, "Perspectives on Professional Women," *Stanford Law Review* 40 (1988): 1163, 1193–94, which notes courts' deference to employers' judgments.

27. This is a complex argument that requires more elaboration than the limits of this article permit. Suffice it to state the obvious: we are experiencing a retreat from public life on many levels, evidenced by, among other factors, declining voter turnout. See also Lani Guinier, "More Democracy," *University of Chicago Legal Forum* (1995): 16–22.

28. *Harper v. Virginia Board of Elections,* 383 US 684 (1966) (Harlan, J., dissenting).

29. See *United States v. Louisiana,* 225 F. Supp. 353, 355–56 (E. D. La. 1963). The decision found that the interpretation test as a prerequisite for registration "has been the highest, best-guarded, most effective barrier to Negro voting in Louisiana," and that the test "has no rational relation to measuring the ability of an elector to read and write," aff'd., 380 US 145 (1965).

30. *Reynolds v. Sims,* 377 US 533, 544 (1964).

DERRICK BELL / *Love's Labor Lost?*
Why Racial Fairness Is a Threat to Many White Americans

1. See, for example, David R. Roediger, *The Wages of Whiteness: Race and the Making of the American Working Class* (London/New York: Verso, 1991); Howard Winant, *Racial Conditions: Politics, Theory, Comparisons* (Minneapolis: University of Minnesota Press, 1994); Noel Ignatiev, *How the Irish Became White* (New York: Routledge, 1995); Jane Lazarre, *Beyond the Whiteness of Whiteness: Memoir of a White Mother of Black Sons* (Durham, N.C.: Duke University Press, 1996); Toni Morrison *Playing in the Dark: Whiteness and the Literary Imagination* (Cambridge: Harvard University Press, 1992); Ian F. Haney Lopez, *White by Law: The Legal Construction of Race* (New York: New York University Press, 1995); and Eric J. Sundquist, *To Wake the Nations: Race in the Making of American Literature* (Cambridge: Belknap/Harvard, 1993).

2. Cheryl Harris, "Whiteness as Property," *Harvard Law Review* 106 (1993): 1707, 1713.

3. Ibid., 1759.

MARY C. WATERS AND CAROLYN BOYES-WATSON /
The Promise of Diversity

1. Peter V. Marsden, "Selection Methods in US Establishments," *Acta Sociologica* 37 (1994): 287–301.

2. David Karen, "Achievement and Ascription in Admission to an Elite College: A Political-Organizational Analysis," *Sociological Forum* 6 (1991): 349–80.

3. Kevin Cullen, "Breaking the Thin Blue Line of Bias: Policewoman Is Likely Next Chief in Springfield," *Boston Globe*, 16 January, 1996.

4. Philip Moss and Chris Tilly, "Soft Skills and Race," *Work and Occupations* 23 (1996): 252–76. See also Kathryn Neckerman and Joleen Kirshcenman, "Hiring Strategies, Racial Bias, and Inner-City Workers: An Investigation of Employers' Hiring Decisions," *Social Problems* 38 (1991): 433–47.

PAUL OSTERMAN/*Too Formal?*

1. William G. Bowen and Derek Bok, *The Shape of the River: Long-Term Consequences of Considering Race in College and University Admissions* (Princeton: Princeton University Press, 1998).

PETER CAPPELLI / *What's Fair?*

1. Harry Holzer and David Neumark, "Assessing Affirmative Action," *Journal of Economic Literature* 38 (2000): 483–95.
2. William T. Dickens and Thomas J. Kane, "Racial Test Score Differences as Evidence of Reverse Discrimination: Less Than Meets the Eye," *Industrial Relations* 38 (1999): 331–63.

SUSAN STURM AND LANI GUINIER / *Reply*

1. See Walter M. Haney, George F. Madaus, and Robert Lyons, *The Fractured Marketplace for Standardized Testing* (Boston: Kluwer Academic Publishing, 1993).
2. See Susan Sturm, "Second Generation Employment Discrimination: A Structural Approach" (*Columbia Law Review,* April 2001). Lani Guinier has undertaken a related exploration of public discourse and democratic practice. See Lani Guinier and Gerald Torres, *The Miner's Canary: Rethinking Race and Power* (forthcoming, Harvard University Press).
3. These examples, and their implications for the regulation of workplace bias, are developed more fully in Sturm, "Second Generation Employment Discrimination" (*Columbia Law Review,* April 2001).

ABOUT THE CONTRIBUTORS

DERRICK BELL is the author of many books, including *And We Are Not Saved* and *Faces at the Bottom of the Well*. He is a visiting professor at New York University Law School.

CAROLYN BOYES-WATSON is associate professor of sociology and director of the Center for Restorative Justice at Suffolk University.

PETER CAPPELLI is director of the Center for Human Resources at the University of Pennsylvania's Wharton School.

HOWARD GARDNER teaches psychology at the Harvard Graduate School of Education. He is author of *Multiple Intelligences, Intelligence Reframed,* and *The Disciplined Mind.*

LANI GUINIER is professor of law at Harvard Law School. She is author of the *Tyranny of the Majority* and *Lift Every Voice,* and co-author of *Becoming Gentlemen.* She and Susan Sturm are the principal investigators for the Racetalks project, funded by the Mott Foundation.

DEBORAH M. KOLB teaches at the Center for Gender in Organizations at the Simmons Graduate School of Management.

PAUL OSTERMAN is professor at MIT's Sloan School of Management and the author of *Securing Prosperity.*

MICHAEL J. PIORE is David W. Skinner Professor of Political Economy at MIT.

PETER SACKS is author, most recently, of *Standardized Minds: The High Price of America's Testing Culture and What We Can Do to Change It.*

MAUREEN A. SCULLY teaches at the Center for Gender in Organizations at the Simmons Graduate School of Management.

ABOUT THE CONTRIBUTORS

CLAUDE M. STEELE is Lucie Stern Professor in the Social Sciences at Stanford University. His articles have appeared in the *New York Times* and *The American Prospect*.

STEPHEN STEINBERG is author of *The Ethnic Myth* and *Turning Back: The Retreat from Racial Justice in American Thought and Policy*.

SUSAN STURM is professor of law at Columbia Law School and the co-principal investigator, with Lani Guinier, of the Racetalks project, funded by the Mott Foundation. Her recent work focuses on normative and regulatory responses to workplace bias.

MARY C. WATERS is professor of sociology at Harvard University and the author of *Black Identities: West Indian Immigrant Dreams and American Realities*.